GNVQ Core Skills

INFORMATION TECHNOLOGY

GNVQ Core Skills

INFORMATION TECHNOLOGY

Intermediate/Advanced

SECOND EDITION

Trevor Arden

PITMAN PUBLISHING

PITMAN PUBLISHING
128 Long Acre, London WC2E 9AN

A Division of Pearson Professional Limited

First published in Great Britain in 1994
Second edition 1995

© Trevor Arden 1994, 1995

The right of Trevor Arden to be identified as Author
of this Work has been asserted by him in accordance
with the Copyright, Designs and Patents Act 1988.

ISBN 0 273 62054 1

British Library Cataloguing in Publication Data
A CIP catalogue record for this book can be obtained from the British Library

All rights reserved; no part of this publication may be reproduced, stored
in a retrieval system, or transmitted in any form or by any means, electronic,
mechanical, photocopying, recording, or otherwise without either the prior
written permission of the Publishers or a licence permitting restricted copying
in the United Kingdom issued by the Copyright Licensing Agency Ltd,
90 Tottenham Court Road, London W1P 9HE. This book may not be lent,
resold, hired out or otherwise disposed of by way of trade in any form
of binding or cover other than that in which it is published, without the
prior consent of the Publishers.

10 9 8 7 6 5 4 3 2 1

Typeset by M Rules
Printed and bound in Great Britain by Clays Ltd, St Ives plc

The Publishers' policy is to use paper manufactured from sustainable forests.

Contents

1 Introduction   1

Core skills in Information Technology Level 2 (Intermediate) • Core skills in Information Technology Level 3 (Advanced) • Activity mapping table

2 Word processing   24

Background to word processing • Situation • Software for word processing • Word processor features • Hardware for word processing • Activities 2.1–2.7

3 Operating systems   46

Definition • Background to MS–DOS • MS–DOS • Activities 3.1–3.3

4 Desktop publishing   58

Background to desktop publishing • Software for desktop publishing • Desktop publishing features • Situation • Hardware for desktop publishing • Activities 4.1–4.7

5 Spreadsheet   81

Background to spreadsheet • Example applications • The structure of a spreadsheet • Activities 5.1–5.9

6 Drawing   111

Background to drawing • Drawing software • Applications of drawing software • Hardware for drawing programs • Features offered by drawing programs • Activities 6.1–6.8

7 Microsoft Windows   131

Definition • Versions • Background to 'Windows' • 'Program Manager' • 'Windows' • 'File manager' • Other 'Windows' accessories • Activity 7.1

8 Database   140

Background to database • Software for database • Situation • Basic features of database • Operation of database • Hardware for database • Activities 8.1–8.8

9 Communications   168

Background to communications • Modem communications • Bulletin boards • Electronic mail (Email) on BT's 'Telecom Gold' • The Internet • Activities 9.1–9.5

10 Charts   186

Background to charts • Software for charts • Hardware for chart drawing • Activities 10.1–10.11

11 Presentations   213

Background to presentations • Software for presentations • Hardware for presentations • Activities 11.1–11.3

12 People and computers   223

Health and safety issues • Data security • Data privacy • Activities 12.1–12.4

13 Hardware for information technology   238

Introduction to information technology (IT) • Advantages and disadvantages of IT • Data • Central processing unit • Processor types • Floppy disks • Hard disk storage • Optical disc storage •

Upgrading • Monitor • Keyboard • Mainframe computers • Mid-range computers • Printing devices

14 Integrating applications 259
Background to integration • Activity 14.1 • Mail merge • Activity 14.2

15 Glossary of terms 269

Index 277

1 Introduction

Core skills in information technology (IT) are a required element of the BTEC GNVQ programmes at levels 2 (Intermediate) and 3 (Advanced). This text covers all the skills required at both levels, through a wide range of computer-based activities. Each activity specifies the performance criteria covered; some are at Intermediate level, some are at Advanced level and some may be attempted by students at either level.

Each chapter covers a specific area of information technology; most chapters focus on a particular software application, with background information on the application together with activities to assess the student's skill. There are several additional areas to put the skill building activities into their context, including 'People and Computers' and 'Hardware'.

Before you attempt each activity, you must:

- find out the precise software program which is available on your computer system;
- if possible, run through a tutorial package to learn the basics of the program;
- make notes where necessary of the precise methods of carrying out the operations required by the activity.

There are enough activities on each area to cover a range of applications for each individual skill. It will be the joint responsibility of the student and the assessor to record and regularly review the student's progress in achievement of skills.

The performance criteria for skills at each level are shown on the following pages.

Core skills in Information Technology (level 2)

Element 2.1: Prepare information

The student selects information appropriate to the task and enters it into software so that it is easy to edit, correcting errors noticed on entry. The student makes decisions about the most appropriate way to store the input and makes backup copies. The student puts right any simple equipment faults and keeps the source information for reference.

Element 2.2: Process information

The student finds the information required for the task and edits and reorganises it as appropriate. The student uses numerical information to make calculations. The student combines information from different sources, editing the result to resolve differences in format. The student saves work regularly.

Element 2.3: Present information

The student considers alternative ways of presenting and displaying information and selects the way which best meets requirements. The student presents combined information, ensuring that the format is consistent. The student produces hard copy of the information, stores the information in files and makes backup copies.

Element 2.4: Evaluate the use of information technology

The student explains the reasons for the use of information technology and compares its use, by her/himself and by others, with other methods. The student describes the software facilities used, evaluates the effects on users of errors and faults and explains the importance of safe working practices.

Element 2.1: Prepare information

PERFORMANCE CRITERIA

A student must:

1 **select information** appropriate to the task
2 **enter information** into **software** in ways that will make it easy to edit
3 keep source **information** required for the task
4 **store input systematically** and make backup copies

RANGE

Select: information taken from existing sources, information developed during input

Information: text, graphics, numbers

Enter: inputting source information accurately, making immediate corrections to errors noticed on entry, putting right simple equipment faults, using manuals and on-line help facilities, asking for help as appropriate

Software: for text, for graphics, for numbers

Store input systematically: naming files sensibly to indicate the contents, locating files conveniently for subsequent use, creating and using directories to group related files, saving work before and after important changes, saving work when all the information has been input

EVIDENCE INDICATORS

For the input of at least two examples each of text, graphics and numbers:

- samples of source information selected
- sample print-outs of what has been input, with annotations to show how the information was input to make it easy to edit
- backup copies of files and print-outs of relevant file directory entries to show how input has been stored systematicaly.

Records of observation by the assessor of the student making immediate corrections to errors noticed on entry, putting right any simple equipment faults which occur and regularly saving work.

Evidence should show that the student can select information appropriate to the task, enter it in ways which will make it easy to edit, respond appropriately to errors, and can store input systematically.

The skills in this element should be learned and demonstrated through activities which will enhance students' capacity to perform effectively in vocational settings.

AMPLIFICATION

Tasks (PC1 and PC3) these are activities which are relevant to the settings in which the student is working and where the use of information technology is judged by the student to be necessary or helpful. They will usually involve work which relates to the requirements of all of the elements in the unit and in many cases to other core skills and vocational units. Examples at this level include producing a newsletter incorporating text, pictures and a table of figures; creating a questionnaire and using a database or spreadsheet to enter and process the information collected, leading to graphs and tables to show survey results; producing a poster, publicity material and a personalised mailshot for a fund-raising event, together with a database of helpers and the kinds of help offered.

Existing sources (PC1 range) examples include printed documents such as price lists or catalogues containing information to go into a database, or images to be scanned. Other examples may be written in longhand, such as notes of a meeting to be word-processed or readings from a survey or experiment that need to go into a spreadsheet.

Information developed during input (PC1 range) this is information which does not exist in hard-copy form before input, but is put together during the process of input, for example formulae, drawings, ideas or a letter to be drafted.

Graphics (PC1, PC2 and PC3 range) this includes, for example, pictures, photographs, drawings and scanned images stored digitally, as well as the software tools for creating new images.

Software (PC2) for text, an example is word processing; for graphics, examples are drawing software and painting software; for number work, examples are spreadsheet software and accounts software. Databases could be used to cover both textual and numerical information; desktop publishing could be used to cover both textual and graphical elements.

Easy to edit (PC2) this includes, for example, the appropriate use of returns and tabs, and the use of a suitable numerical format when numbers are used for calculation.

Errors (PC2 range) examples include typing mistakes that can be corrected before the return key is pressed. Other examples are an attempt to input a word instead of a date, or to input a number that is too big.

Simple equipment faults (PC2 range) for example, those caused by poorly connected cables, equipment being switched off or wrongly set up.

Backup copies (PC4) work saved on a separate storage medium, for example, a floppy disc.

GUIDANCE

Tasks, such as gathering and entering information for an article in a newsletter, selecting and entering information into a database about a group of people or products, drawing or scanning pictures to be incorporated in a poster, or entering readings from an experiment into a spreadsheet, should provide students with opportunities to:

- develop skills in selecting and entering different types of information as appropriate to the task and in a way suited to the software in order to facilitate efficient subsequent processing of the information

- develop a systematic approach to storing the information they have input

- learn to recognise errors and faults and respond accordingly

- develop good working practices such as saving information methodically, and showing an awareness of health and safety issues (contributing to the requirements for Element 2.4).

Element 2.2: Process information

PERFORMANCE CRITERIA

A student must:

1 **find information** required for the task

2 use appropriate **software** to **edit information**

3 process numerical **information** by using **software** to make calculations

4 **reorganise information** as required for the task

5 save work at **appropriate intervals**

6 **combine information** from different sources, resolving differences of format

RANGE

Find: by looking in the right directory, by looking for files with a given name, by searching for information which meets specified criteria

Information: text, graphics, numbers

Software: for text, for graphics, for numbers

Edit: amending, moving, reformatting, copying, deleting, inserting

Reorganise: sorting, restructuring stored information

Appropriate intervals: before and after important changes, when the processing is complete

Combine: importing information of the same type, importing information of a different type

EVIDENCE INDICATORS

For the processing of at least two examples each of text, graphics and numbers:

- print-outs of information both before, during and at the end of processing. The print-outs should be annotated to show the effects of using all the editing techniques in the range and reorganising information, and making calculations

- print-outs of information both before and after information has been combined from different sources. This should include print-outs showing at least one example of importing information of the same type and at least one example of importing information of different types. The final print-outs should show the combined information edited into a consistent format.

Records of observation by the assessor of the student finding information and saving work before and after important changes.

Evidence should show that the student can find, edit and reorganise information and make calculations as required for a particular task.

The skills in this element should be learned and demonstrated through activities which will enhance students' capacity to perform effectively in vocational settings.

AMPLIFICATION

Tasks (PC1 and PC4) these are activities which are relevant to the settings in which the student is working and where the use of information technology is judged by the student to be necessary or helpful. They will usually involve work which relates to the requirements of all the elements in the unit and in many cases to other core skills and vocational units. Examples at this level include producing a newsletter incorporating text, pictures and a table of figures; creating a questionnaire and using a database or spreadsheet to enter and process the information collected, leading to graphs and tables

Introduction 5

to show survey results; producing a poster, publicity material and a personalised mailshot for a fund-raising event, together with a database of helpers and the kinds of help offered.

Specified criteria (PC1 range) the search criteria will be specified by the student to meet the requirements of the task, for example 'sex = female and age <25'.

Software (PC2 and PC3) for text, an example is word processing; for graphics, examples are drawing software and painting software; for number work, examples are spreadsheet software and accounts software. Databases could be used to cover both textual and numerical information; desktop publishing could be used to cover both textual and graphical elements. CD-ROM software could be used to provide textual, graphical and numerical information.

Reformatting (PC2 range) this includes both operations on individual items, for example underlining a word or converting a number to currency format, and operations concerning larger collections of information, for example changing paragraph layout, the style of shading in a diagram, or the sizes of columns in a table.

Make calculations (PC3) for example, use a formula in a spreadsheet or total numerical fields in a database.

Sorting (PC4 range) examples include sorting records in a database or rows in a spreadsheet.

Restructuring (PC4 range) examples include changing the sequence in which rows or columns in a spreadsheet are organised, reorganising text under headings and subheadings, reorganising information from a database as required for the task.

Resolving differences of format (PC6) the imported material should look natural in its new location. Examples of differences include different fonts, margins, tab settings, paragraph layouts, sizes and/or shapes of graphics, forms of tables, formats of numbers.

Importing (PC6 range) examples include bringing information from another source into the file being processed, pulling a picture from a drawing file into a desktop-published file of text, using electronic mail to download information into a file.

GUIDANCE

Tasks, such as revising and reorganising material for a newsletter, adding to or changing information in a database, arranging a mailshot for a selected group, amending and combining drawings and text for a poster, or analysing the results of an experiment, should provide students with opportunities to:

- develop skills in processing and combining different types of information, using a range of facilities

- learn to recognise errors and faults and respond accordingly

- develop good working practices such as preventing loss or corruption of information, and showing an awareness of health and safety issues (contributing to the requirements for Element 2.4).

Element 2.3: Present information

PERFORMANCE CRITERIA

A student must:

1 present **information** in different ways and select which way best meets the **requirements** of the task
2 use appropriate **software** to display **information**
3 use appropriate **software** to produce hard copy of **information**
4 present combined **information** in a consistent format
5 store **information** in files and make backup copies

RANGE

Information: text, graphics, numbers

Requirements: fitness for purpose, matched to audience, clarity, accuracy, appropriate use of information referencing, consistent format

Software: for text, for graphics, for numbers

EVIDENCE INDICATORS

For at least two examples of combining information of different types:

- records of observation by the assessor of information displayed on screen
- print-outs of presented combined information
- backup copies of files containing combined information.

Between them, these examples should cover text, graphics and numbers. The information should be displayed and presented so that it meets all of the requirements in the range.

Evidence should also include an example of at least two different ways of presenting the same information, accompanied by an explanation of why one has been selected which best meets requirements.

Evidence should show that the student can present information appropriate to a task in a way which meets requirements.

The skills in this element should be learned and demonstrated through activities which will enhance students' capacity to perform effectively in vocational settings.

AMPLIFICATION

Tasks (PC1) these are activities which are relevant to the settings in which the student is working and where the use of information technology is judged by the student to be

Introduction 7

necessary or helpful. They will usually involve work which relates to the requirements of all of the elements in the unit and in many cases to other core skills and vocational units. Examples at this level include producing a newsletter incorporating text, pictures and a table of figures; creating a questionnaire and using a database or spreadsheet to enter and process the information collected, leading to graphs and tables to show survey results; producing a poster, publicity material and a personalised mailshot for a fund-raising event, together with a database of helpers and the kinds of help offered.

Information referencing (PC1 range) many documents should include references, for example, date, page numbers and titles. These can often be generated automatically.

Software (PC2 and PC3) for text, an example is word processing; for graphics, examples are drawing software and painting software; for number work, examples are spreadsheet software and accounts software. Databases could be used to cover both textual and numerical information; desktop publishing could be used to cover both textual and graphical elements.

Combined information (PC4) this is information in the form of text, graphics and number combined into a consistent format.

Consistent format (PC4) screen display and print-out should be designed so that the information is clear and is arranged in manageable portions. There should be no output across page breaks or perforations of continuous stationery and tables should be easy to read.

Backup copies (PC5) work saved on a separate storage medium, for example, a floppy disc.

GUIDANCE

Tasks, such as producing hard copy of a newsletter or a poster, displaying selected information from a database about a group of people or products, or printing graphs and tables to present the results of an experiment, should provide students with opportunities to:

- develop skills in using information technology to present different types of information, including combined information, using a range of facilities and formats

- explore different ways of presenting information and make judgements about which way best meets requirements

- develop good working practices such as ensuring accuracy of information, and showing an awareness of health and safety issues (contributing to the requirements for Element 2.4).

Element 2.4: Evaluate the use of information technology

PERFORMANCE CRITERIA

A student must:

1   explain the reasons for using information technology

2   **compare** the **methods** used by the student and by others for preparing, processing and presenting information

3   describe the software facilities used to meet the requirements of the task

4 explain the effects on users of **problems** that can occur when using information technology

5 explain the importance of **working safely** and in line with good working practices

RANGE

Compare in terms of: speed, ease of use, effort, accuracy

Methods: manual, alternative ways of using information technology

Problems: errors, equipment faults, loss of information

Working safely: safety of the user, safety of the equipment, safety of the information

EVIDENCE INDICATORS

An explanation of the reasons for using information technology in relation to particular tasks. The explanation should cover both an account of why and how the student has chosen to use information technology and the reasons for the use of information technology by others such as a commercial, industrial or public sector organisation. The explanation should include a comparison of the speed, ease of use, effort and accuracy of using information technology against using manual methods for preparing, processing and presenting the same information for the particular task, together with a description of software facilities used.

A log of errors and faults that occurred with the information technology used during the task with an evaluation of the effects of both errors and equipment faults on the user.

An explanation of working safely and in line with good working practices in relation to the student's use of information technology.

The skills in this element should be learned and demonstrated through activities which will enhance students' capacity to perform effectively in vocational settings.

AMPLIFICATION

Reasons (PC1) examples include making things more effective or easier when processing a large volume of information, when undertaking an activity which will take a long time to perform manually, or when storing large amounts of information.

Software facilities (PC3) these are the tools, operations and methods provided by the software to support the preparation, processing and presentation of information covered in Elements 2.1 to 2.3.

Tasks (PC3) these are activities which are relevant to the settings in which the student is working and where the use of information technology is judged by the student to be necessary or helpful. They will usually involve work which relates to the requirements of all the elements in the unit and in many cases to other core skills and vocational units. Examples at this level include producing a newsletter incorporating text, pictures and a table of figures; creating a questionnaire and using a database or spreadsheet to enter and process the information collected, leading to graphs and tables to show survey results;

producing a poster, publicity material and a personalised mailshot for a fund-raising event, together with a database of helpers and the kinds of help offered.

Errors (PC4 range) for example, inaccurate information, inappropriate processing.

Equipment faults (PC4 range) for example, those caused by poorly connected cables, equipment being switched off or wrongly set up, equipment failing.

Working practices (PC5) examples include lists of Do's and Don'ts such as keeping cables tidy, positioning screens to avoid reflections, keeping drinks away from equipment, storing discs away from heat and electrical equipment. They also include precautions to avoid loss or corruption of information and unauthorised use of information.

GUIDANCE

Tasks, such as creating a newsletter or a poster, selecting, storing and displaying information about a group of people or products, organising a mailshot, or capturing, analysing and presenting the results of an experiment, and investigating the use of information technology by others, should provide students with opportunities:

- to make judgements about the effectiveness and implications of using information technology
- to examine the information needs and methods used in everyday contexts such as supermarkets and libraries
- to consider the use of information technology by others including, as appropriate, ways of using information technology of which the student may not have direct experience, for example, measurement and control applications
- to consider the implications of basic errors and faults, good working practices and health and safety issues.

Core skills in Information Technology (level 3)

Element 3.1: Prepare information

The student selects information appropriate to the task and enters it into software so that it is easy to edit, correcting errors noticed on entry. This includes configuring software to aid input of information. The student makes decisions about the most appropriate way to store the input and makes backup copies. The student puts right any simple equipment faults and keeps the source information for reference.

Element 3.2: Process information

The student finds the information required for the task, including the accessing of remote sources, and edits and reorganises it as appropriate. The student uses numerical information to make calculations. The student combines information from different sources, editing the result to resolve differences in format. The student processes information efficiently through the creation and use of automated routines. The student saves work regularly.

Element 3.3: Present information

The student is systematic in preparing the information to be presented. The student considers alternative ways of presenting and displaying information and selects the way which best meets requirements. The student presents combined information, ensuring that the format is consistent. The student produces hard copy of the information, stores the information in files and makes backup copies.

Element 3.4: Evaluate the use of information technology

The student explains the justifies the reasons for the use of information technology and compares its use, by her/himself and by others, with other methods. The student describes the software facilities used, evaluates the effects on users of errors and faults and explains the importance of safe working practices.

Element 3.1: Prepare information

PERFORMANCE CRITERIA

A student must:

1 **select information** appropriate to the task

2 **enter information** into **software** in ways that will make it easy to edit

3 keep source **information** required for the task

4 **store input systematically** and make backup copies

5 **configure software** to aid input of **information**

RANGE

Select: information taken from existing sources, information developed during input

Information: text, graphics, numbers

Enter: inputting source information accurately, making immediate corrections to errors noticed on entry, putting right simple equipment faults, using manuals and on-line help facilities, asking for help as appropriate

Software: for text, for graphics, for numbers

Store input systematically: naming files sensibly to indicate the contents, locating files conveniently for subsequent use, creating and using directories to group related files, saving work before and after important changes, saving work when all the information has been input

Configure software: creating style sheets for text input, creating spreadsheet templates, creating database structures

EVIDENCE INDICATORS

For the input of at least two examples each of text, graphics and numbers:

- samples of source information selected
- sample print-outs of what has been input, with annotations to show how the information was input to make it easy to edit
- backup copies of files and print-outs of file directories showing how the files containing the information which has been input have been named to give an indication of their content and organised into directories.

Print-outs of at least one example each of style sheets, spreadsheet templates and database structures which the student has created.

Records of observation by the assessor of the student making immediate corrections to errors noticed on entry, putting right any simple equipment faults which occur and regularly saving work.

Evidence should show that the student can select information appropriate to the task, enter it in ways which will make it easy to edit, configure software to aid input, respond appropriately to errors, and can store input systematically.

The skills in this element should be learned and demonstrated through activities which will enhance students' capacity to perform effectively in vocational settings.

AMPLIFICATION

Tasks (PC1 and PC3) these are activities which are relevant to the settings in which the student is working and where the use of information technology is judged by the student to be necessary or helpful. They will usually involve work which relates to the requirements of all of the elements in the unit and in many cases to other core skills and vocational units. Examples at this level include producing, with the aid of automated routines, a newsletter incorporating information from a variety of sources and showing evidence of design intended to match the audience and achieve maximum impact; creating a questionnaire and using a database or spreadsheet to enter and analyse the information collected, leading to a report incorporating graphs and tables; producing a poster, publicity material and a personalised mailshot for a fund-raising event, together with a database or spreadsheet to assist planning and management of the event by scheduling activities, keeping track of helpers and accounting for expenditure and income.

Existing sources (PC1 range) examples include printed documents such as price lists or catalogues containing information to go into a database, or images to be scanned. Other examples may be written in longhand, such as notes of a meeting to be word-processed or readings from a survey or experiment that need to go into a spreadsheet.

Information developed during input (PC1 range) this is information which does not exist in hard-copy form before input, but is put together during the process of input, for example formulas, drawings, ideas or a letter to be drafted.

Graphics (PC1 range) this includes, for example, pictures, photographs, drawings and scanned images stored digitally, as well as the software tools for creating new images.

Software (PC2) for text, an example is word processing; for graphics, examples are drawing software and painting software; for number work, examples are spreadsheet software and accounts software. Databases could be used to cover both textual and numerical information; desktop publishing could be used to cover both textual and graphical elements.

Easy to edit (PC2) this includes, for example, the appropriate use of returns and tabs, and the use of a suitable numerical format when numbers are used for calculation.

Errors (PC2 range) examples include typing mistakes that can be corrected before the return key is pressed. Other examples are an attempt to input a word instead of a date, or to input a number that is too big.

Simple equipment faults (PC2 range) for example, those caused by poorly connected cables, equipment being switched off or wrongly set up.

Backup copies (PC4) work saved on a separate storage medium, for example, a floppy disc.

Style sheets (PC5 range) these are structures which provide a standard layout, for example, a memo form for use in word processing.

Spreadsheet templates (PC5 range) these are spreadsheets which can be used repeatedly whereby the structure is retained but some information is altered; examples include invoices and order forms.

Database structures (PC5 range) the database structure includes input screens with field sizes and types which may be automatically checked when information is entered.

GUIDANCE

Tasks, such as preparing and entering information for a newsletter, a database, a mailshot, a poster, a survey, an experiment or a financial model, involving the discriminating use of information technology tools and techniques to aid the effectiveness of the work, should provide students with opportunities to:

- develop skills in selecting and entering different types of information as appropriate to the task and in a way suited to the software in order to facilitate efficient subsequent processing of the information
- configure software to aid this work
- develop a systematic approach to storing the information they have input
- learn to recognise errors and faults and respond accordingly
- develop good working practices such as saving information methodically, and showing an awareness of health and safety issues (contributing to the requirements for Element 3.4).

Element 3.2: Process information

PERFORMANCE CRITERIA

A student must:

1 **find information** required for the task

2 use appropriate **software** to **edit information**

3 process numerical **information** by using **software** to **make calculations**

4 **reorganise information** as required for the task

5 save work at **appropriate intervals**

6 **combine information** from different sources, resolving differences of format

7 create automated routines that aid efficient processing of **information**

RANGE

Find: by looking in the right directory, by looking for files with a given name, by searching for information which meets specified criteria, by accessing remote sources

Information: text, graphics, numbers

Software: for text, for graphics, for numbers

Edit: amending, moving, reformatting, copying, deleting, inserting

Make calculations: by creating totals in databases or spreadsheets, by using formulas incorporating absolute and relative references to spreadsheet cells

Reorganise: sorting, restructuring stored information

Appropriate intervals: before and after important changes, when the processing is complete

Combine: importing information of the same type, importing information of a different type

EVIDENCE INDICATORS

For the processing of at least two examples each of text, graphics and numbers:

- print-outs of information both before, during and at the end of processing. The print-outs should be annotated to show the effects of using all the editing techniques in the range and reorganising information, and making calculations

- print-outs of information both before and after information has been combined from different sources. This should include print-outs showing at least one example of importing information of the same type and at least one example of importing information of different types. The 'after' print-outs should show the combined information edited into the same format.

Print-outs of at least two examples of different automated routines which the student has created. Records of observation by the assessor of the student finding information and saving work before and after important changes.

Evidence should show that, in completing a particular task, the student can process and combine information of different types and create automated routines to help. The skills in this element should be learned and demonstrated through activities which will enhance students' capacity to perform effectively in vocational settings.

AMPLIFICATION

Tasks (PC1) these are activities which are relevant to the settings in which the student is working and where the use of information technology is judged by the student to be necessary or helpful. They will usually involve work which relates to the requirements of all the elements in the unit and in many cases to other core skills and vocational units. Examples at this level include producing, with the aid of automated routines, a newsletter incorporating information from a variety of sources and showing evidence of design intended to match the audience and achieve maximum impact; creating a questionnaire and using a database or spreadsheet to enter and analyse the information collected, leading to a report incorporating graphs and tables; producing a poster, publicity material and a personalised mailshot for a fund-raising even, together with a database or spreadsheet to assist planning and management of the event by scheduling activities, keeping track of helpers and accounting for expenditure and income.

Specified criteria (PC1 range) the search criteria will be specified by the student to meet the requirements of the task, for example 'sex = female and age <25'.

Remote sources (PC1 range) these include information held on other computers, accessed via a network or by telecommunication.

Software (PC2 and PC3) for text, an example is word processing; for graphics, examples are drawing software and painting software; for number work, examples are spreadsheet software and accounts software. Databases could be used to cover both textual and numerical information; desktop publishing could be used to cover both textual and graphical elements. CD-ROM software could be used to provide textual, graphical and numerical information.

Reformatting (PC2 range) this includes both operations on individual items, for example underlining a word or converting a number to currency format, and operations concerning larger collections of information, for example changing paragraph layout, the style of shading in a diagram, or the sizes of columns in a table.

Absolute and relative references (PC3 range) an example is the processing of an order, where the cost of the items in any particular row of the spreadsheet is calculated as the unit cost of the item (relative reference, because it relates to this item) times the number of items ordered (another relative reference) increased by the VAT rate (absolute reference to the cell where the current rate for the relevant class of items is stored).

Sorting (PC4 range) for example, sorting records in a database or rows in a spreadsheet.

Restructuring (PC4 range) for example, changing the sequence in which rows or columns in a spreadsheet are organised, reorganising text under headings and subheadings, reorganising information from a database as required for the task.

Resolving differences of format (PC6) the imported material should look natural in its new location. Examples of differences include different fonts, margins, tab settings, paragraph layouts, sizes and/or shapes of graphics, forms of tables, formats of numbers.

Importing (PC6 range) for example, bringing information from another source into the file being processed, pulling a picture from a drawing file into a desktop-published file of text, using electronic mail to download information into a file.

Automated routines (PC7) these are tools which allow repetitive sequences of operations to be programmed into single operations, for example macros, batch files, programmable keys and icons, mail-merge, database query and report routines.

GUIDANCE

Tasks, such as editing, reorganising and analysing information relating to a newsletter, a database, a poster, a mailshot, a survey, an experiment or a financial model, involving the discriminating use of information technology tools and techniques to aid the effectiveness of the work, should provide students with opportunities to:

- develop skills in processing and combining different types of information, using a range of facilities
- create routines which can be used repeatedly in order to make processing more effective
- learn to recognise errors and faults and respond accordingly
- develop good working practices such as preventing loss or corruption of information, and showing an awareness of health and safety issues (contributing to the requirements for Element 3.4).

Element 3.3: Present information

PERFORMANCE CRITERIA

A student must:

1 **prepare information** for presentation

2 present **information** in different ways and select which way best meets the **requirements** of the task

3 use appropriate **software** to display **information**

4 use appropriate **software** to produce hard copy of **information**

5 present combined **information** in a consistent format

6 store **information** in files and make backup copies

RANGE

Prepare: selecting the form and content of the information to match the requirements of the task, date-stamping and paginating documents, using named directories for associated display files, storing successive developments of information for presentation with version numbers and informative file names

Information: text, graphics, numbers

Requirements: fitness for purpose, matched to audience, clarity, accuracy, consistent format

Software: for text, for graphics, for numbers

EVIDENCE INDICATORS

For the presentation of at least two examples of combining different types of information:

- records of observation by the assessor of information displayed on screen
- print-outs of presented combined information
- backup copies of files containing combined information.

Between them, these examples should cover text, graphics and numbers. The information should be displayed and presented so that it meets all of the requirements in the range.

Evidence should also include an example of at least two different ways of presenting the same information, accompanied by an explanation of why one has been selected which best meets requirements.

Evidence should show that in relation to a particular task the student can organise information for presentation.

The skills in this element should be learned and demonstrated through activities which will enhance students' capacity to perform effectively in vocational settings.

AMPLIFICATION

Selecting (PC1 range) the form and content of the information to be presented requires the application of design skills, taking into account for example the desired impact of the product, the appropriate balance of 'white space' with text, tables and illustrations, the logical presentation of information, as well as more detailed aspects of layout.

Version numbers (PC1 range) examples include automated version numbering systems for file names or the use of names like PIC1 and PIC2 which help to show the sequence of development of a drawing.

File names (PC1 range) as far as possible, file names should convey information about the content and purpose of the file.

Tasks (PC2) these are activities which are relevant to the settings in which the student is working and where the use of information technology is judged by the student to be necessary or helpful. They will usually involve work which relates to the requirements of all of the elements in the unit and in many cases to other core skills and vocational units. Examples at this level include producing, with the aid of automated routines, a newsletter incorporating information from a variety of sources and showing evidence of design intended to match the audience and achieve maximum impact; creating a questionnaire and using a database or spreadsheet to enter and analyse the information collected, leading to a report incorporating graphs and tables; producing a poster, publicity material and a personalised mailshot for a fund-raising event, together with a database or spreadsheet to assist planning and management of the event by scheduling activities, keeping track of helpers and accounting for expenditure and income.

Software (PC3 and PC4) for text, an example is word processing; for graphics, examples are drawing software and painting software; for number work, examples are spreadsheet software and accounts software. Databases could be used to cover both textual and numerical information; desktop publishing could be used to cover both textual and graphical elements.

Combined information (PC5) this is information in the form of text, graphics and number combined into a consistent format.

Consistent format (PC5) screen display and print-out should be designed so that the information is clear and is arranged in manageable portions. There should be no output across page breaks or perforations of continuous stationery and tables should be easy to read.

Backup copies (PC6) work saved on a separate storage medium, for example, a floppy disc.

GUIDANCE

Tasks, such as producing a newsletter, a display of information from a database, a poster, a mailshot, a report of results from a survey or an experiment, or an analysis of a financial model, involving the discriminating use of information technology tools and techniques to aid the effectiveness of the work and matching the presentation to the audience, should provide students with opportunities to:

- prepare systematically the information which is to be presented
- develop skills in using information technology to present different types of information, including combined information, using a range of facilities and formats
- explore different ways of presenting information and make judgements about which way best meets requirements
- develop good working practices such as ensuring accuracy of information, and showing an awareness of health and safety issues (contributing to the requirements for Element 3.4).

Element 3.4: Evaluate the use of information technology

PERFORMANCE CRITERIA

A student must:

1. explain and justify the reasons for using information technology
2. **compare** the **methods** used by the student and by others for preparing, processing and presenting information
3. **evaluate** alternative **systems** for managing information
4. describe the software facilities used to meet the requirements of the task
5. explain the effects on users of **problems** that can occur when using information technology
6. explain the importance of **working safely** and in line with good working practices

RANGE

Compare in terms of: speed, ease of use, effort, accuracy

Methods: manual, alternative ways of using information technology

Evaluate: effectiveness, cost, effects on employment, benefits (to individuals, to organisations), disadvantages (to individuals, to organisations)

Systems: manual, information technology

Problems: system faults, errors, equipment faults, loss of information

Working safely: safety of the user, safety of the equipment, safety of the information

EVIDENCE INDICATORS

An explanation and justification of the reasons for using information technology in relation to particular tasks. The explanation should cover both an account of why and how the student has chosen to use information technology and the reasons for the use of information technology by others such as a commercial, industrial or public sector organisation. The explanation should include a comparison of the speed, ease of use, effort and accuracy of using information technology against using manual methods for preparing, processing and presenting the same information for the particular task, together with a description of software facilities used.

A short report evaluating at least three examples of systems for managing information comparing IT-based methods and non IT-based methods.

A log of errors and faults that occurred with the information technology used during the task with an evaluation of the effects of software faults, equipment faults and system faults on the user.

An explanation of working safely and in line with good working practices in relation to the student's use of information technology.

The skills in this element should be learned and demonstrated through activities which will enhance students' capacity to perform effectively in vocational settings.

AMPLIFICATION

Reasons (PC1) examples include making things more effective or easier when processing a large volume of information, when undertaking an activity which will take a long time to perform manually, or when storing large amounts of information.

Systems (PC3) evaluating a system includes considering the purpose and the effects of using information technology within the wider context of the application, as well as examining the way the system works.

Effectiveness (PC3 range) the effectiveness of a system includes, for example, the extent to which it meets a perceived need, offers new or improved ways of using information, is 'user-friendly' and is integrated within the wider context.

Individuals and organisations (PC3 range) there is a contrast between the views of the organisation, of the users of the services provided by the organisation, and of others. An important consideration is proper control of the use of sensitive information, an area where data protection legislation applies.

Software facilities (PC4) these are the tools, operations and methods provided by the software to support the preparation, processing and presentation of information covered in Elements 3.1 to 3.3.

Tasks (PC4) these are activities which are relevant to the settings in which the student is working and where the use of information technology is judged by the student to be necessary or helpful. They will usually involve work which relates to the requirements of all the elements in the unit and in many cases to other core skills and vocational units. Examples at this level include producing, with the aid of automated routines, a newsletter incorporating information from a variety of sources and showing evidence of design intended to match the audience and achieve maximum impact; creating a questionnaire and using a database or spreadsheet to enter and analyse the information collected, leading to a report incorporating graphs and tables; producing a poster, publicity material and a personalised mailshot for a fund-raising event, together with a database or spreadsheet to assist planning and management of the event by scheduling activities, keeping track of helpers and accounting for expenditure and income.

System faults (PC5 range) these are to do with mismatches between the design of the system and what it is required to do; examples of faults in major systems feature regularly in the press and provide a useful source for learning.

Errors (PC5 range) for example, inaccurate information, inappropriate processing, failure of software to deal with exceptional situations.

Equipment faults (PC5 range) for example, those caused by poorly connected cables, equipment being switched off or wrongly set up, equipment failing.

Working practices (PC6) examples include lists of Do's and Don'ts such as keeping cables tidy, positioning screens to avoid reflections, keeping drinks away from equipment, storing discs away from heat and electrical equipment. They also include precautions to avoid loss or corruption of information and unauthorised use of information, the prevention or detection and removal of viruses, and a proper respect for copyright of software.

GUIDANCE

Tasks, such as creating a newsletter, a database of information about a group of people or products, a poster, a mailshot, a report resulting from a survey or an experiment, or an analysis of a financial model, involving the discriminating use of information technology tools and techniques to aid the effectiveness of the work, and investigating the use of information technology by others, should provide students with opportunities to:

- make judgements about the effectiveness and implications of using information technology
- evaluate systems used for managing information within their own work and in everyday contexts such as supermarkets and libraries
- evaluate the use of information technology by others including, as appropriate, ways of using information technology of which the student may not have direct experience, for example, measurement and control applications
- consider the implications of basic errors and faults, good working practices and health and safety issues.

Activity mapping table

Use this mapping table to find activities which cover the four elements of the core skills:

Element 1: Prepare information

Element 2: Process information

Element 3: Present information

Element 4: Evaluate the use of information technology

Chapter 2   Word processing

Activity	Level	I.T. Core Skill Elements	Page
2.1	INT	PREPARE	31
2.2	INT	PREPARE	34
2.3	INT	PREPARE / PROCESS / PRESENT	36
2.4	INT	PREPARE / PROCESS / PRESENT	38
2.5	ADV	PREPARE	40
2.6	ADV	PREPARE / PRESENT	42
2.7	ADV	PREPARE / PRESENT	44

Chapter 3   Operating systems

Activity	Level	I.T. Core Skill Elements	Page
3.1	INT	PROCESS	50
3.2	INT & ADV	PROCESS	53
3.3	ADV	PROCESS	55

Chapter 4   Desktop publishing

Activity	Level	I.T. Core Skill Elements	Page
4.1	INT	PRESENT	65
4.2	INT	PRESENT	66
4.3	INT	PRESENT	68
4.4	INT	PRESENT	69
4.5	INT & ADV	PREPARE / PROCESS / PRESENT	73
4.6	ADV	PREPARE / PROCESS / PRESENT	75
4.7	ADV	PREPARE / PROCESS / PRESENT	77

Chapter 5   Spreadsheet

Activity	Level	I.T. Core Skill Elements	Page
5.1	INT	PREPARE / PROCESS	88
5.2	INT	PREPARE / PROCESS / PRESENT	90
5.3	INT	PREPARE / PROCESS / PRESENT	93
5.4	INT & ADV	PREPARE / PROCESS	95
5.5	INT & ADV	PREPARE / PROCESS / PRESENT	97
5.6	INT & ADV	PREPARE / PROCESS / PRESENT	100
5.7	ADV	PREPARE / PROCESS	103
5.8	ADV	PREPARE / PROCESS / PRESENT	105
5.9	ADV	PREPARE / PROCESS / PRESENT	108

Chapter 6	Drawing		
Activity	*Level*	*I.T. Core Skill Elements*	*Page*
6.1	INT	PROCESS / PRESENT	119
6.2	INT	PROCESS / PRESENT	120
6.3	INT	PROCESS / PRESENT	121
6.4	INT	PROCESS / PRESENT	123
6.5	ADV	PROCESS / PRESENT	124
6.6	ADV	PROCESS / PRESENT	125
6.7	ADV	PROCESS / PRESENT	127
6.8	ADV	PROCESS / PRESENT	129

Chapter 7	Microsoft Windows		
Activity	*Level*	*I.T. Core Skill Elements*	*Page*
7.1	INT & ADV	PROCESS	137

Chapter 8	Database		
Activity	*Level*	*I.T. Core Skill Elements*	*Page*
8.1	INT	PREPARE / PROCESS / PRESENT	149
8.2	INT	PREPARE / PROCESS / PRESENT	151
8.3	INT & ADV	PREPARE / PROCESS / PRESENT	153
8.4	INT & ADV	PREPARE / PROCESS / PRESENT	156
8.5	INT & ADV	EVALUATE	159
8.6	ADV	EVALUATE	160
8.7	ADV	PREPARE / PROCESS / PRESENT / EVALUATE	162
8.8	ADV	PREPARE / PROCESS / PRESENT / EVALUATE	165

Chapter 9	Communications		
Activity	*Level*	*I.T. Core Skill Elements*	*Page*
9.1	INT & ADV	PREPARE / PROCESS	174
9.2	INT & ADV	PREPARE / PROCESS / PRESENT	177
9.3	INT & ADV	PROCESS / EVALUATE	179
9.4	ADV	PROCESS / EVALUATE	182
9.5	ADV	PREPARE / PROCESS / PRESENT	183

Chapter 10	Charts		
Activity	*Level*	*I.T. Core Skill Elements*	*Page*
10.1	INT	PREPARE / PRESENT	190
10.2	INT	PREPARE / PRESENT	192
10.3	INT	PREPARE / PRESENT	194
10.4	INT	PREPARE / PRESENT	196
10.5	INT & ADV	PREPARE / PRESENT	197
10.6	INT & ADV	PREPARE / PROCESS / PRESENT	199
10.7	ADV	PREPARE / PROCESS / PRESENT	201
10.8	INT & ADV	PREPARE / PRESENT	204
10.9	INT & ADV	PREPARE / PRESENT	206
10.10	ADV	PREPARE / PROCESS / PRESENT	208
10.11	ADV	PREPARE / PROCESS / PRESENT	210

Chapter 11	Presentations		
Activity	*Level*	*I.T. Core Skill Elements*	*Page*
11.1	INT & ADV	PREPARE / PRESENT	217
11.2	INT & ADV	PREPARE / PRESENT	219
11.3	ADV	PREPARE / PRESENT	220

Chapter 12	People and computers		
Activity	*Level*	*I.T. Core Skill Elements*	*Page*
12.1	INT & ADV	PREPARE / PRESENT / EVALUATE	231
12.2	INT & ADV	PREPARE / PRESENT / EVALUATE	233
12.3	INT & ADV	PREPARE / PRESENT / EVALUATE	235
12.4	ADV	PRESENT / EVALUATE	236

Chapter 14	Integrating applications		
Activity	*Level*	*I.T. Core Skill Elements*	*Page*
14.1	INT & ADV	PREPARE / PROCESS / PRESENT	260
14.2	ADV	PREPARE / PROCESS / PRESENT	264

2 Word processing

Background to word processing

Word processing is the use of computers for the production of documents which contain mainly text. A word-processing system consists of three elements: the software (programs); the hardware (equipment such as computer and printer); and the user.

Situation

For some of the activities later in this chapter, you are to take on the role of the Assistant Leisure Officer at the Sportstown Leisure Centre. This is a job which involves you in a variety of activities, some of them administrative. The Centre Manager, Ian Whicker, wants the centre to increase its use of computers, as he thinks that this will improve efficiency and give a better image to our customers. The Leisure Centre is equipped with several personal computers (PCs), and your current task is to improve your own ability to produce, edit and print word-processed documents. Read the following information before you do the activities.

Software for word processing

There is a wide range of word-processing software available for personal computers. Some of the best-known programs are:

- Word Perfect

- Lotus Ami Pro
- Microsoft Word
- Wordstar

■ DOS or Windows version

Most word processor software is available in two forms – in MS–DOS version or as a Windows version. The MS–DOS version can be run on any standard PC, with or without the Windows interface, but the Windows version will not operate without the Microsoft Windows software. (See Chapter 3 on 'Operating systems' and Chapter 7 on Microsoft 'Windows'.)

Word processor features

A word processor is not simply an advanced form of typewriter. Although electronic typewriters are commonplace, and have their uses, they do not do the same job as word processors. The basic features of a word processor are:

■ On-screen edit before print

Text can be typed at the keyboard and edited on screen before any printing takes place. This feature allows the typist to type at a faster speed, without having to worry about typing mistakes. The mistakes can be corrected once the document is finished.

■ Save to disk

Documents can be saved on disk for calling up in the future and using again. In addition, multiple copies of documents may be printed.

■ Spell checker

Words can be checked for correct spelling. This feature should be used with care, since not all errors in a document will necessarily show up as spelling mistakes. The power of this feature depends upon the size of the dictionary which the software has access to. The larger the dictionary, the more efficient the spelling checker will be.

The user may find that the spell checker works slowly. This is because, for every word in the document to be checked, the computer must search through the very large number of words held in the dictionary on disk. Clearly, this takes time, and so the more powerful the computer, the more effective will be the use of the spell checker.

■ Grammar checker

Sentence construction and grammar can be checked. This is available with some word processor software, or it may be used as a separate program on a document which has already been created and stored on disk in a file.

■ Thesaurus

A Thesaurus may be used to find alternative words of similar meaning.

■ Fonts

Many different fonts (character styles) may be used. The particular font in use determines the precise shapes of all the printed characters; in addition the size of the font may be varied, and some of the text can be emboldened, underlined or italicised.

■ Page layout

Page layouts, including the setting of margins, indents, line spacing and tab stops can be changed very easily and quickly. In this way you can use the word processor to experiment with the layout of the text in a document until you reach a layout which is satisfactory.

■ Template files

A specific layout can be kept in a file on disk (sometimes called a template or style sheet) so that the same layout can be applied to a number of different documents. This could ensure that all the documents have the same margins, indents, paper sizes, fonts, company name, address and logo, for example. A standard document layout is often required in business, especially if the document is to go out to customers. This is sometimes called a house style. The Sportstown Leisure Centre could adopt a house style for all its leaflets and letters promoting activities.

■ Search and replace

A searching facility allows the user to search for each (or the next) occurrence of a particular word (or number of words) in a document. If required, a word which is searched for and found can be replaced automatically by another word.

At Sportstown Leisure Centre a *Guide to the Leisure Centre* was produced several years ago. When Ian Whicker was appointed as manager in place of the previous manager John Farnborough, the search and replace facility was used to replace every reference to 'John Farnborough' by 'Ian Whicker'. This saved considerable time in editing.

There are many other features available in word processors which can be useful in everyday work on document production, such as the ability to include pictures in documents, create an index to a longer document, sort list of names alphabetically, and draw lines, boxes and other shapes on the screen.

Hardware for word processing

The items of hardware which are essential to a typical word processing system are:

- Personal computer
- Keyboard
- Mouse
- Monitor (this may be a colour or monochrome screen)
- Hard disk drive (capacity 200Mb or more), which is inside the CPU box
- Floppy disk drive (capacity 720Kb or 1.44Mb), which is at the front of the CPU box
- Printer

The list shows a typical hardware specification to run a word processing system. There are, however, many variations to this specification, depending mainly on the requirements for the job.

Fig. 1 Word processing system

■ Processor

The personal computer is defined mainly by its processor. This processor may be a 286, 386SX, 386DX, 486SX, 486DX or Pentium. The list gives the names of the processor in order of power (and expense). Most of today's word processor software can be run on any of these processors, but the earlier ones (286 and 386) will run the software more slowly than the later ones (486 and Pentium).

It can be an advantage to use a computer with a more powerful processor if you are using very recently produced word processor software, since, on the earlier processors, there may be an annoying delay in instructions given with the keyboard or mouse actually being carried out and changing the text on the screen. This is particularly true of 'WYSIWYG' (What you see is what you get) word processors. With this type of word processor, the text (and possibly pictures and diagrams) which is on the screen is an exact match to the text which will print on paper. Ideally, all word processors would be WYSIWYG, since the user is primarily concerned with what his/her document will actually look like on paper. For now, however, this is not always the case.

At Sportstown Leisure Centre, the PCs are used for a variety of tasks. Some are used mainly for word processing, but others are also used to keep records of bookings of the main hall, badminton, tennis and squash courts. The number of bookings for all the various activities at the Leisure Centre made in one day is very large, so you can see that there is a lot of information which must be stored on the computer systems. In addition, the computers need to keep a record of payments for all the bookings, so that accounts can be kept up to date.

It is very common to find that PCs are used not just for one task (such as word processing), but for a variety of tasks. The hardware needs to be sufficiently powerful to support all the tasks, not just one.

Another important point about hardware is that, in a business situation, the uses that a computer is put to frequently change. Even though the PCs at Sportstown Leisure Centre are used only for word processing at the moment, it is very likely that their use will change in the future. A PC which is currently running just word processing may be used to run accounts and database applications in the future. Therefore, hardware systems need to be flexible. Ian Whicker, the Manager, needs to keep an eye to the future when he is deciding on hardware specifications today.

In summary, the particular processor in use will affect the operation of the word processor software; however, the processor in use is not as important to the efficient use of the word processor software as it is for other applications such as desktop publishing, databases and graphics.

■ Monitor

The monitor may be a simple, standard resolution monochrome monitor, which would adequately display the text of a document. However, colour monitors are more convenient for software which has been designed to work in colour, and if an individual is working with the computer for a significant amount of time each day, is better to use a monitor with a higher resolution; that is, one which produces a sharper image on the screen. For a full-time secretary at the Leisure Centre who is constantly using the computer for typing letters and other documents, or for updating records of booking and classes, it is desirable that the monitor in use provides the clearest possible image, with no tendency to produce eye strain or headaches. (For information on health and safety factors, refer to Chapter 12, 'People and computers'.)

■ Disk storage

Typical hard disk drives in use with word processing systems range in capacity from 200Mb to 800Mb. Much larger capacities are available for applications which need them. The capacity, measured in megabytes (roughly millions of bytes) determines how much information can be stored on the hard disk.

The information to be stored on disk for word processing comes in two forms. First, the word processing software will need to be stored on the hard disk. Modern PC software is large in size, due to its complexity, and may take up between 10Mb and 35Mb. It is likely that the computer in use for word processing will also be needed for other applications (such as storing accounts files or supplier details), and so room on the hard disk has to be made available for this.

In addition to the software, the documents you produce also have to be stored somewhere; although these can be kept on floppy disk it is often more convenient (and faster) to store them on the hard disk. The amount of room taken up by documents purely depends on the number and size of documents being stored.

■ Printer

There are many types of printer available (see Chapter 13). Which particular type is used depends upon the documents which are to be produced. Whereas some documents are needed in draft form only, others must be attractively presented, with a variety of formatting styles.

For example, an internal memorandum, while it needs to be clear and well-presented, is basically a simple message from one person to another, and so there is no need to spend a long time making it look attractive. On the other hand, a leaflet which is used to advertise a new sporting activity at the Leisure Centre is to be read by members of the public. These are potential customers for the Leisure Centre, and so it is important not only that the leaflet is accurate and clear, but also that it is eye-catching and will encourage the reader to keep reading and follow up the information given.

A dot matrix printer will provide for the minimum word-processing requirements in most situations. An impact dot matrix printer is noisy, and this may be a nuisance in the Leisure Centre's administrative office, and for this reason the office is equipped with ink-jet printers, which are nearly silent in operation. In addition there is a laser printer available for work which has to be of a very high quality, and, in this situation, designs, logos and diagrams are included in documents along with normal text.

Because laser printers are relatively expensive to buy (and run), Ian Whicker has asked the staff to use the ink-jets for normal work, and the laser only for final copies of leaflets and other material for the public. This is typical of many office work places at present.

▶▶ FIND OUT

1 Find out what word processing software you are to use. Find out also how to run the word processor program on your system. The method of running the program will be simple, but the precise method depends on how your system has been set up. In addition, you will need access to a user manual, tutorial package and any other form of help which is available.

2 Find out whether a laser printer is available to you, what type it is, and what the rules are regarding its use. If you are working on a network, the laser printer may be in a different location to the computer you are working on.

Activity 2.1

SITUATION

The Centre Manager, Ian Whicker, has asked you to produce a document on the word processor.

CONTENTS

Enter text; insert and delete text in a document; save a file to disk; use a spell checker and a visual check to find and correct any errors in data entry.

Level: INTERMEDIATE

Element: PREPARE INFORMATION

TASKS

1 Run the word processor software.

2 Key in the following text as accurately as you can:

Sportstown Leisure Centre Open Day : 27 July 1995

Sportstown Leisure Centre has been purpose-built on the Hudson Way site, and was officially opened on 1 August 1989. It is well equipped, with a large main hall providing the central facility. The main hall is extremely flexible in use; it can support 8 badminton/short tennis courts, or alternatively 2 basketball/indoor football or hockey courts. The hall can be divided with ultra-modern 'easy-pull' partitions, so that different sports can be offered simultaneously.

Other activities in the main hall which have taken place recently include trampolining, roller skating, roller disco, indoor cricket and even boxing. Our internationally acclaimed viewing and refreshment facilities allow the most prestigious national and international events to be staged – a glance at our list of events last year will confirm this.

The 6 squash courts are all Perspex-backed, allowing clear viewing of games from the stepped viewing gallery. We are particularly keen to encourage youngsters to take up squash, and, to this end, we offer free coaching to under-14s every Saturday morning during school term time.

Finally, there is the fitness centre – our latest addition to the centre. All weight training and multi-gym equipment is available, and we encourage all shapes, sizes and ages to come along for a free assessment of your 'fitness needs'.

3 Save the document to your own disk or to your own user area under the file name OPENDAY1. (When you save the file the word processor you are using will add a 3-character file name extension. Word Perfect, for example, may store the file as OPENDAY1.WPS or OPENDAY1.WPF. This is done so that the word processor software is able to find word-processing documents from amongst a list of files some of which were created using other software, such as spreadsheet or graphics.)

4 Print the text.

5 At the end of the first paragraph, change 'simultaneously' to 'concurrently'.

6 Delete the word 'recently' from the first line of the second paragraph.

7 Insert the word 'crystal' before 'clear' in the third paragraph.

8 Add the following as an extra paragraph at the end of the text.

The Leisure Centre is a facility for all the family. We really do hope you will find the time to come along to our open day. There will be plenty of helpful staff on hand to answer any questions you may have, and if you want to become a member, or simply to make bookings on a casual basis, we shall be pleased to accommodate you.

9 Use the spell checker facility and also check your spelling and grammar visually on the screen. Make any corrections that are required.

10 Save the new version under the same file name (overwriting the previous file). Also make a back-up copy of the file under a different name.

11 Print the final version of the text. In your own handwriting, neatly label the changes you have made from the first version of the document.

12 List on screen, and then, print on paper, the files in the current directory, including the file names for this activity.

13 Exit the word processor.

Activity 2.2

SITUATION

The Centre Manager, Ian Whicker, has asked you to produce a document on the word processor.

CONTENTS

Enter text; insert and delete text in a document; save a file to disk; use a spell checker and a visual check to find and correct any errors in data entry.

Level: INTERMEDIATE

Element: PREPARE INFORMATION

TASKS

1 Run the word processor program.

2 Key in the following text:

Sportstown Leisure Centre Squash Club

Join our squash club! We have a Club Night on Tuesday evening from 6.00pm–9.30pm. This is open to all, and all standards of players are welcome, from beginners to professionals! In fact the aims are to improve your standard and to enjoy a chat with other players at the same time. The evening costs only £3, and, depending on numbers on any particular night, you could be on court for up to 2 hours – obviously a bargain.

If you join the squash club you will automatically be placed in the leagues. We currently have 12 divisions, with 6 players in each division. Each division lasts one month, so you play 5 league games each month. The scoring system is explained on the squash club noticeboard. At the end of the month we use a 'two up, two down' method of shuffling players between the divisions. This means that you quickly find your own level – then it's up to you to maintain it or improve.

The cost of joining the Squash Club is only £25. This includes a booking card at the reduced rate of £9 – it would normally cost you £12. (The booking card entitles you to book courts by telephone up to seven days in advance.) So don't delay – join today!

3 Save to your own disk or to your own user area under the file name SQUASH1.

4 Print the text.

5 In paragraph 1, change 'professionals' to 'experts'.

6 Delete the word 'currently' from the second paragraph.

7 Insert 'Sportstown' before 'Squash Club' in the third paragraph.

8 Add the following paragraph to the end of the text.

Coaching is available every Monday and Wednesday evening between 6.00pm and 8.00pm. The coach is our club professional, Jason Khan, and he charges £12 per half-hour for an individual student, or £6 each per half-hour for two students on court together. Please leave your name at reception if you are interested.

9 Use the spell check facility and also check your spelling and grammar visually on the screen.

10 Save the new version under the file name (overwriting the previous file). Also make a back-up copy of the file under a different file name.

11 Print the final version of the text. In your own handwriting, neatly label the changes you have made from the first version of the document.

12 List on screen, and then print on paper, the files in the current directory, including the file names for this activity.

13 Exit the word processor.

Activity 2.3

SITUATION

The Centre Manager, Ian Whicker, has asked you to retrieve a document on the word processor so that it can be amended.

CONTENTS

Recall a document from your disk or user area; apply character formatting to selected areas of text; edit document layout; preview printed document before printing on paper.

Level: INTERMEDIATE

Elements: PREPARE, PROCESS, PRESENT INFORMATION

TASKS

1 Run the word processor program.

2 Retrieve the OPENDAY1 file from your disk or user area.

3 Make the following changes to the layout and character formatting of the document, as shown below:

   (a) insert a new line between the heading and the body of the text;

   (b) embolden and centre the heading;

   (c) embolden the words 'purpose-built', 'coaching' and 'free assessment', as shown in the text below;

   (d) make a new paragraph starting with 'There will be plenty . . .' as shown in the text below.

Sportstown Leisure Centre Open Day : 27 July 1995

Sportstown Leisure Centre has been **purpose-built** on the Hudson Way site, and was officially opened on 1 August 1989. It is well equipped, with a large main hall providing the central facility. The main hall is extremely flexible in use; it can support 8 badminton/short tennis courts, or alternatively 2 basketball/indoor football or hockey courts. The hall can be divided with ultra-modern 'easy-pull' partitions, so that different sports can be offered simultaneously.

Other activities in the main hall which have taken place recently include trampolining, roller skating, roller disco, indoor cricket and even boxing. Our internationally acclaimed viewing and refreshment facilities allow the most prestigious national and international events to be staged – a glance at our list of events last year will confirm this.

The 6 squash courts are all Perspex-backed, allowing clear viewing of games from the stepped viewing gallery. We are particularly keen to encourage youngsters to take up squash, and, to this end, we offer free **coaching** to under-14s every Saturday morning during school term time.

Finally, there is the fitness centre – our latest addition to the centre. All weight training and multi-gym equipment is available, and we encourage all shapes, sizes and ages to come along for a **free assessment** of your 'fitness needs'.

The Leisure Centre is a facility for all the family. We really do hope you will find the time to come along to our open day.

There will be plenty of helpful staff on hand to answer any questions you may have, and if you want to become a member, or simply to make bookings on a casual basis we shall be pleased to accommodate you.

4   Change the document to double line spacing. Preview the printed form of the document for A4 paper and make any adjustment necessary.

5   Save the new version under the file name OPENDAY2. Also make a back-up copy of the file under a different file name.

6   Print the final version of the text. In your own handwriting, neatly label the changes you have made from the first version of the document.

7   List on screen, and then print on paper, the files in the current directory, including the file names for this activity.

8   Exit the word processor.

Activity 2.4

SITUATION

The Centre Manager, Ian Whicker, has asked you to retrieve a document on the word processor so that it can be amended.

CONTENTS

Recall a document from disk; apply character formatting to selected areas of text; edit document layout; preview printed document before printing on paper.

Level: INTERMEDIATE

Elements: PREPARE, PROCESS, PRESENT INFORMATION

TASKS

1 Run the word processor program.

2 Retrieve the SQUASH1 file from your disk or user area.

3 Make the following changes to the layout and character formatting of the document, as shown below:

   (a) insert a new line between the heading and the body of the text;

   (b) embolden and centre the heading;

   (c) embolden the words 'all standards of players are welcome', 'leagues' (paragraph 2) and 'booking card' (paragraph 3, second sentence), as shown in the text below;

   (d) Make a new paragraph starting with 'The scoring system is explained . . .' as shown in the text below.

Sportstown Leisure Centre Squash Club

Join our squash club! We have a Club Night on Tuesday evening from 6.00pm–9.30pm. This is open to all, and **all standards of players are welcome**, from beginners to experts! In fact the aims are to improve your standard and to enjoy a chat with other players at the same time. The evening costs only £3, and, depending on numbers on any particular night, you could be on court for up to 2 hours – obviously a bargain.

If you join the squash club you will automatically be placed in the **leagues**. We have 12 divisions, with 6 players in each division. Each division lasts one month, so you play 5 league games each month.

The scoring system is explained on the squash club noticeboard. At the end of the month we use a 'two up, two down' method of shuffling players between the divisions. This means that you quickly find your own level – then it's up to you to maintain it or improve.

The cost of joining the Sportstown Squash Club is only £25. This includes a **booking card** at the reduced rate of £9 – it would normally cost you £12. (The booking card entitles you to book courts by telephone up to seven days in advance.) So don't delay – join today!

Coaching is available every Monday and Wednesday evening between 6.00pm and 8.00pm. The coach is our club professional, Jason Khan, and he charges £12 per half-hour for an individual student, or £6 per hour for two students on court together. Please leave you name at reception if you are interested.

4   Change the document to double line spacing. Preview the printed form of the document for A4 paper and make any adjustment necessary.

5   Save the new version under the file name SQUASH2. Also make a back-up copy of the file under a different name and on a different drive (such as floppy disk).

6   Print the final version of the text. In your own handwriting, neatly label the changes you have made from the first version of the document. Also explain briefly on the printout why the document may be more effective in double line spacing.

7   List on screen, and then print on paper, the files in the directories you have used, including the file names for this activity.

8   Exit the word processor.

Activity 2.5

SITUATION

The Centre Manager, Ian Whicker, has asked you to produce a memo on the word processor. This should be done using the layout shown.

CONTENTS

Enter text; centre, underline and embolden selected text; save a file to disk; use a spelling checker and a visual check to find and correct any errors in data entry; change selected text to a different font.

Level: ADVANCED

Element: PREPARE INFORMATION

TASKS

1 Run the word processor program.

2 Key in the following text in single line spacing, ensuring that you use the correct procedure on the word processor to centre the two heading lines. Also, use the tab key to set out the position of the words 'Ref' and 'Date'.

Sportstown Leisure Centre

MEMORANDUM

To: All staff   Ref: Computer systems

From: General Manager   Date: 12 January 1995

As you all know, we have invested quite heavily in some new computer equipment recently. I know that in the past the centre has been run without the use of computer systems to any great extent, and I feel that it is time we adopted a more business-like approach to all areas of administrative work. The centre will be able to respond to enquiries and prepare information much more quickly with our new systems, but this, of course, depends on you (and me!).

We need to be fully confident in using the computers, and this can only come from a thorough knowledge of how all the procedures are dealt with on the computer system. For this reason, I am putting aside a significant amount of money from this year's budget to spend on computer training. The aim is for all staff who make use of the computer systems to be fully trained within 6 months.

Please arrange an interview with me in the next couple of weeks to discuss your individual training needs. Thanks for your co-operation.

3 Embolden the two heading lines, and underline the text shown as underlined in the memo above.

4 Use the spelling checker and a visual on-screen check to find and correct any errors. If your word processor allows it, use the grammar checker to verify that Ian's sentence construction is adequate!

5 Save the file to your disk or user area under the file name: MEMO1. Make a backup file to disk (under a different file name) in case of accidental loss. Preview and then print the memo.

6 Change the margins for the document to 1 inch top and bottom, 1.5 inch left margin and 1 inch right margin.

7 Save the new version under the same file name (overwriting the previous file). Also make a back-up copy of the file under a different file name.

8 Print the final version of the text. In your own handwriting, neatly label

the changes you have made from the first version of the document.

9 List on screen, and then print on paper, the files in the current directory, including the file names for this activity.

10 Select and then cut (or delete) all the "data" in the memorandum. You should now be left with a blank memorandum template which can be kept for future use. Save this template under a suitable file name, and then print the blank memorandum.

11 Exit the word processor.

Activity 2.6

SITUATION

The Centre Manager, Ian Whicker, has asked you to produce an activities price list. This should be done using the layout shown below.

CONTENTS

Use the tab stops to help produce a table of information on the word processor; save a file to disk; use a visual check; change font size to fit on paper.

Level: ADVANCED

Elements: PREPARE, PRESENT INFORMATION

TASKS

1 Run the word processor program.

2 Examine the table below, and (if necessary) set tab stops on the word processor so that the table can be set out as shown. Set the tab stops for the columns which show money so that they are right-aligned at the tab position. In this way, the decimal places will all be underneath one another, which is the correct procedure. Set the tab stop for the column 'Length of session' so that the information is centred at the tab position.

3 Using the tab stop positions which you have set, key in the following table of Sportstown Leisure Centre prices. Use single line spacing. The heading should be emboldened and centred.

Sportstown Leisure Centre Prices (£s)

Activity	Length of session	Charge Mon–Fri Daytime	Charge Mon–Fri Evening	Charge Sat–Sun Day/Evening
Badminton	45 min	2.50	3.00	2.50
Short tennis	45 min	2.50	3.00	2.50
Squash	45 min	3.50	4.00	3.50
Table tennis	30 min	2.00	2.50	2.00
Multi-gym	30 min	3.50	5.00	3.50
Basketball	1 hour	25.00	30.00	30.00
Indoor football	1 hour	25.00	30.00	30.00
Indoor hockey	1 hour	25.00	30.00	30.00
Running track	2 hours	2.00	2.00	2.00
Hire of hall	1 hour	35.00	40.00	40.00
Hire of half-hall	1 hour	20.00	30.00	30.00

4 Verify that the data has been keyed in accurately by doing a visual on-screen check. Make changes as required to correct any errors.

5 Preview the printout. If the table will not fit on a single page, change the font to a smaller point size until it does fit the paper.

6 Save the document under the file name PRICES1. Also make a back-up copy of the file under a different file name.

7 Print the final version of the document. In your own handwriting, neatly label the positions in the document where you have placed tabs.

8 List on screen, and then print on paper, the files in the current directory, including the file names for this activity.

9 Select and then cut (or delete) all the numbers in the table. You should now be left with a blank template which can be kept for future use. Save this template under a suitable file name, and then print the blank table.

10 Exit the word processor.

Activity 2.7

SITUATION

The Centre Manager, Ian Whicker, has asked you to produce a staff rota. This should be done using the layout shown below.

CONTENTS

Use the tab stops to help produce a table of information on the word processor; save a file to disk; use a visual check; change font size to fit on paper.

Level: ADVANCED

Elements: PREPARE, PRESENT INFORMATION

TASKS

1 Run the word processor program.

2 Examine the table below, and (if necessary) set tab stops on the word processor so that the table can be set out as shown. Set the tab stops for the columns which show staff names so that they are centred at the tab position.

3 Using the tab stop positions which you have set, key in the following table showing the Staff Rota for Reception. Use double line spacing. The heading should be emboldened and centred.

Staff Rota for Reception
Week 4 1995

	8am–1pm	1pm–6pm	6pm–11pm
Monday	B Smythe	D Gibson	J Higgins
Tuesday	B Smythe	J Higgins	D Gibson
Wednesday	B Smythe	J Higgins	D Gibson
Thursday	Y Murray	J Higgins	D Gibson
Friday	Y Murray	D Gibson	S Cottle
Saturday	Y Murray	D Gibson	S Cottle
Sunday	S Cottle	B Smythe	S Cottle

4 Verify that the data has been keyed in accurately by doing a visual on-screen check. Make changes as required to correct any errors.

5 Preview the printout, in both landscape and portrait modes. Select the most appropriate mode. If the table does not fit on a single page, change the font to a smaller point size until it does fit the paper.

6 Save the document under the file name ROTA1. Also make a back-up copy of the file under a different file name and on a different drive.

7 Print the final version of the document. In your own handwriting, neatly label the positions in the document where you have placed tabs. Also explain briefly on the printout why you have chosen either landscape or portrait mode.

8 Select and then cut (or delete) all the names in the table. You should now be left with a blank template which can be kept for future use. Save this template under a suitable file name, and then print the blank table.

9 List on screen, and then print on paper, the names of the file in the current directories you have used, including the file names for this activity.

10 Exit the word processor.

3 Operating systems

Definition

The operating system of a computer is a set of programs which provide a means of communication between the hardware and the user of the computer. Computer operating systems include :

- Windows 95
- MS–DOS (Microsoft Disk Operating System)
- OS/2 (an IBM operating system for personal computers)
- UNIX (originally for mainframes, but now available in versions for mid-range and personal computers)
- CP/M (the predecessor of MS–DOS)

The majority of personal computers use MS–DOS, and this is the one which will be emphasised in this book. If your system uses a different operating system, some details will be different, but you will still be able to carry out the activities.

Background to MS–DOS

The Microsoft Disk Operating System in a number of different versions, is installed on millions of computers worldwide. The operating system is required to be run in the PC before any further processing can take place. When the computer is switched on, the operating system boots up from the hard disk or the network disk drive. The meaning of this is that a number of programs are run to prepare the computer for further use, and part of the operating system software must remain resident in the random access memory (RAM) of the computer.

The function of the operating system is to act as a link between the hardware of the central processing unit and the software which the user intends to operate. For this reason, all applications programs (such as word processors, spreadsheets and databases) for PCs have been written for the specific operating system to be used; in most cases this is MS–DOS.

MS–DOS has been released in a number of different versions. Each version differs from the previous one in terms of the features it offers and the way it is used. Most applications software which is available will work not only with the current version of MS–DOS, but also with at least some of the previous versions.

The user is not necessarily aware of the operating system while he or she is using applications software. However, the operating system software is working away continuously all the time the computer is in use. Specifically, the operating system deals with requests from the applications program to use various parts of the hardware of the computer, such as the interface for sending data to a printer, or the interface for refreshing the screen image. Even while the computer is switched on but lying idle, the operating system will be active, regularly checking the keyboard to see if a key has been pressed.

Examples of functions of the operating system of a computer are as follows.

■ Deal with input data

The operating system ensures that the computer checks the keyboard of a PC to see which key (if any) has been pressed by the user. If a key has been pressed, it returns a particular code number which represents a keyboard character such as a letter 'A', a digit '4' or a cursor control movement such as the up arrow. This character is then dealt with by the operating system; it may be displayed on the screen, or it may be passed to the applications program which is currently being run, to produce some effect within the program.

The operating system deals with data as it is input from other devices, such as floppy disk drives. Data from a disk file must be stored in the current memory (RAM) of the computer until it is ready to be dealt with by the program currently in use. The operating system will check (as far as it is able) for any errors which appear in the data as it is loaded from disk. If errors are spotted, the program or the user will be informed, so that corrective action can be taken.

■ Data transmission

When requested by the user, usually through an applications program such as a word processor, data has to be sent from the main memory (RAM) of the computer to another device. This device will be connected to one of the interfaces (or ports) of the computer, and the operating system will ensure that the data is sent to the right interface at the right speed so that it reaches the device successfully. An example of this process is the sending of a word processor file to a printer. The data will be sent to the correct parallel or serial port, from where it will print on the printer. If the printer is off line (not accepting data), the operating system will send a message back to the word processor program, which, in turn, will tell the user via the screen that something is wrong.

■ Dealing with errors

Many types of errors can occur during processing on a computer system. It is the job of the operating system to deal with these errors in such a way that the user can put the errors right and then continue to use the computer. Examples of errors which are dealt with by the operating system are:

- The printer is off line.
- The required file is not found on the disk.
- The memory is full.
- The wrong key has been pressed.

■ Manage the memory resources of the computer

The computer has two types of memory which are continually in use: first, the internal memory, or RAM (random access memory); and secondly, disk storage. When an application program is in use, there is usually not enough room to store all the program in RAM, and so only those parts of the program which are currently needed are in RAM at any one time. The rest of the program remains on disk. There is a continual movement of programs (and data) between RAM and disk memory, and this is dealt with by the operating system. In addition, the operating system must ensure that programs or data in RAM and on disk are kept safe and are not overwritten by other data or programs if they are still needed.

The management of memory resources is complicated, and it is one of the most important tasks for the operating system to perform. The user is not generally aware of this process, but, nevertheless, if he or she is to work with a computer system with the minimum of problems, he or she ought to have an idea of what is happening to the programs and data.

There are hundreds of other tasks for the operating system to perform, most of which go on in the background. Tasks involving the operating system which the user is generally aware of mostly involve what might be called housekeeping operations, such as file management.

■ File management

Functions of the operating system which the user may be aware of are those which involve file management, such as:

- Listing the names of files on the floppy disk.
- Copying files from one disk to another, or from one area to another.
- Deleting files which are no longer required.
- Checking on certain aspects of files, including their size and when they were last updated.
- Making new sub-directories on a disk in order to keep a large number of files organised under headings.
- Using batch files, which are used to store and execute automatically short sequences of commands.

MS-DOS

MS-DOS versions 5 and 6 can be accessed from the operating system prompt:

    C:>_

The prompt is all that appears on the screen (apart from previous data).

This is rather daunting for the beginner to MS–DOS, and is one of the reasons why users often avoid typing in commands at this stage. They may prefer to give commands either through MS–DOS Shell, or through Microsoft Windows, both of which provide a graphical user interface. This allows the user to operate a mouse and/or pull-down menus to select operations instead of having to type them from their own memory or from a reference manual. It is thought by most people that this makes the operating system much easier to use.

Activity 3.1 Listing files in MS–DOS

SITUATION

You are to use a number of MS–DOS commands in order to view files on disk drives. If your system uses a different operating system, carry out the same operations, but note that the format of the commands will be totally different.

CONTENTS

Log onto various disk drives; obtain lists of files in different formats, on screen and on a printer; view the properties and contents of files.

Level: INTERMEDIATE

Element: PROCESS INFORMATION

TASKS

1. Return your computer system to the MS–DOS command line prompt. You should see **C:>_** or a similar prompt on the screen.

2. Type **cls** and then press **<Enter>** to clear the screen of any previous information.

3. Place a formatted floppy disk in the drive. We shall assume that the drive you are using is drive A. (If it is drive B, change each A to B in the tasks that follow.)

Type:

A: <Enter>

4 The computer is now accessing the floppy disk drive A as the currently selected drive. (Other drives may be available on your system, for example, drive C or D, which are the usual names for the hard disk drives, or drives called by any other capital letter, which may be network drives. Whichever drive is required as the current drive, you simply type its name followed by a colon and then press **<Enter>**.)

5 Type:

dir   <Enter>

to obtain a list of all the files and sub-directories on drive A in the currently selected directory. Note the information which the command displays:

- the file name (up to 8 characters);
- the file name extension (usually 3 characters);
- the file size (in bytes);
- the date the file was last amended;
- the time the file was last amended.

Some of the items in the list may be sub-directories rather than actual files. These will have **<Dir>** next to them.

At the bottom of the file list is displayed the number of files in the list and an indication of the amount of space remaining on the disk for the storage of further files.

6 If the list of files is a long one which will not fit on the screen, the list will quickly disappear off the top of the screen, and you will not have time to see some of the file names.

To display a list of files a page (screenful) at a time, type:

dir /p   <Enter>

The list first screenful will be displayed, with a message 'Press any key to continue' at the bottom.

7 An alternative to this is to type:

dir /w   <Enter>

This will give a 'wide' display of the file names only, not showing the file size and last amendment date and time. This is useful if you are looking for a particular file amongst a large number of files in a directory.

8 Press the function key F3 **<Enter>**. This repeats on the screen the last MS–DOS command that you entered (the 'keyboard buffer'), and can be a useful time saver.

9 Look at your list of files. Pick one file name out (a word processor file if possible) and display its contents as a text file by typing:

    type <filename>   <Enter>

where **<filename>** is the full name (including the 3-letter file name extension) of the file whose contents you have chosen to display. For example, if you have a file in the list called LETTER1.WPS, then you should type:

    type letter1.wps   <Enter>

This will show the contents of the file as if it were a pure text file. With some files this will work, and you will be able to see what is in the file even though the layout will not be correct. With other files – for example graphics files – the contents will appear to be garbage. The command can be useful for checking MS–DOS file contents.

10 Occasionally, you need a printed version of the information which is displayed on the screen from these MS–DOS commands. This is done by typing, for example:

    dir > prn   <Enter>

which directs the output from the **dir** command to the printer instead of the screen. Note that a printer must be attached and on line for the command to work.

11 Finish this session in MS–DOS by showing your tutor/lecturer that you can carry out all the operations in this activity.

Activity 3.2 Using sub-directories in MS–DOS

SITUATION

You are to use a number of MS–DOS commands in order to work with directory structures on disk drives. If your system uses a different operating system, carry out the same operations, but note that the format of the commands will be totally different.

CONTENTS

Move between different directories of a disk; view a directory tree structure; make new sub-directories.

Levels: INTERMEDIATE, ADVANCED

Element: PROCESS INFORMATION

TASKS

1 Return your computer system to the MS–DOS command line prompt. You should see:

> **C:>_**

or a similar prompt on the screen.

2 Type **cls** and then press **<Enter>** to clear the screen of any previous information.

3 Place a formatted floppy disk in the drive. We shall assume that the drive you are using is drive A. (If it is drive B, change each A to B in the tasks that follow.)

Type

> **A: <Enter>**

4 The computer is now accessing the floppy disk drive A as the currently selected drive. (Other drives may be available on your system, for example, drive C or D, which are the usual names for the hard disk drives, or drives called by any other capital letter, which may be network drives. Whichever drive is required as the current drive, you simply type its name followed by a colon and then press **<Enter>**.)

5 Type:

dir <Enter>

This will display the list of files in the currently selected directory. Now make a new sub-directory called 'myfiles'. To do this, type:

md myfiles <Enter>

The command means 'make a sub-directory called "myfiles"'.

A sub-directory is simply a heading under which other files can be grouped.

Type:

dir <Enter>

to see the directory name listed with the files which were already there.

6 Go into the sub-directory **myfiles**, and create two further sub-directories called 'letters' and 'sheets'. To do this, type:

cd myfiles <Enter>

(This means 'change the current directory to **myfiles**'.)

md letters <Enter>

md sheets <Enter>

7 Go back a directory level by typing:

cd.. <Enter>

8 Display the directory 'tree' structure which you have created by typing:

tree <Enter>

If this does not work, try the following:

c:\dos\tree <Enter>

or

path c:\dos <Enter>

tree <Enter>

9 Finish this session in MS–DOS by showing your tutor/lecturer that you can carry out all the operations in this activity.

Activity 3.3 Copying and renaming files

SITUATION

You are required to copy and rename some files in different directories on disk.

CONTENTS

Copy and rename files; view lists of files on screen and printer.

Level: ADVANCED

Element: PROCESS INFORMATION

TASKS

1 Return your computer system to the MS–DOS command line prompt. You should see **C:>**_ or a similar prompt on the screen.

2 Type:

   cls   <Enter>

to clear the screen of any previous information.

3 Place a formatted floppy disk in the drive. We shall assume that the drive you are using is drive A. (If it is drive B, change each A to B in the tasks that follow.)

Type:

   A: <Enter>

4 The computer is now accessing the floppy disk drive A as the currently selected drive. (Other drives may be available on your system, for example, drive C or D, which are the usual names for the hard disk drives, or drives called by any other capital letter, which may be network drives. Whichever drive is required as the current drive, you simply type its name followed by a colon and then press **<Enter>**.)

5 Type:

   dir   <Enter>

Operating systems   55

This will display the list of files in the currently selected directory.

Ensure that you are in the same directory, on the same disk as in the previous activity. If not, change disk and/or directory until you have the sub-directory **myfiles**, with its further sub-directories' letters and sheets. The aim of this activity will be to copy files from the current (root) directory into the sub-directories which you previously created.

6 Pick out and note down the names of four files from the list of files in the current directory. Assuming that they are called **file1.ext**, **file2.ext**, **file3.ext** and **file4.ext**, carry out the following commands:

    copy file1.ext   myfiles\letters   <Enter>

    copy file2.ext   myfiles\letters   <Enter>

    copy file3.ext   myfiles\sheets   <Enter>

    copy file4.ext   myfiles\sheets   <Enter>

(Note that you must use your exact file names instead of **file1.ext, file2.ext** and so on.)

These commands should have copied the four files given, two into the sub-directory called **letters**, and two into the sub-directory called **sheets**. The original files have been left where they were.

7 Check that the files have been copied into the right directories by using the **cd** (change directory) and **dir** (list files) commands.

8 Move into the sub-directory called **letters**, and rename the first file you copied into this directory as **first.xxx** by typing:

    rename file1.ext first.xxx

List the files in this directory to the printer.

9 Move into the sub-directory called sheets, and rename the first file you copied into this directory as **second.yyy** by typing:

    rename file3.ext second.yyy

List the files in this directory to the screen, and then to the printer.

10 Finish the session with MS–DOS.

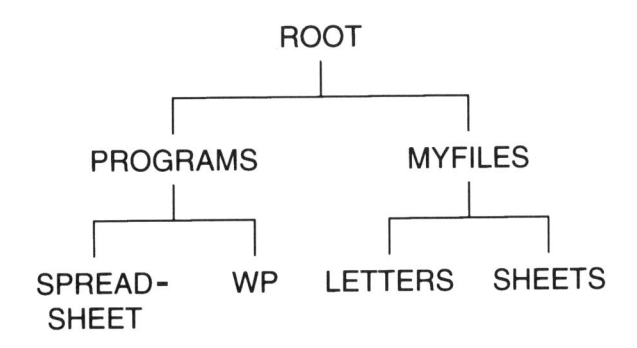

```
                        ROOT
            ┌────────────┴────────────┐
        PROGRAMS                   MYFILES
         ┌──┴──┐                   ┌───┴───┐
      SPREAD-   WP              LETTERS  SHEETS
      SHEET
```

Fig. 2 Directory tree

4 Desktop publishing

Background to desktop publishing

Desktop publishing (DTP) is the use of a personal computer for the production of documents which may contain both pictures and typed text. The DTP system does the same job as a word-processing system, but the difference is that with DTP the user can be more particular about the precise position on the printed page of the text and pictures which make up the document.

Whereas you would generally use a word processor to produce a letter, a memo or a report, you would more effectively make use of a DTP program to produce a page for a newsletter or magazine, an advertisement or leaflet. A desktop publishing system consists of three elements: the DTP software, the hardware (with particular emphasis on the printer) and the user. The user has a more difficult role in DTP than in word processing, because production of the end document requires a much greater level of skill and training. In fact, although it is quite possible for a relative beginner to produce fairly simple desktop published documents, the more complex ones require many hours of training and practice.

Software for desktop publishing

There is a wide range of DTP software available for personal computers; some of the best-known programs are:

- Pagemaker

- Ventura Publisher
- Timeworks
- Quark XPress
- Serif Page Plus

>> **FIND OUT**

> **1** Find out what DTP software you are to use. Find out also how to run the DTP program on your system. The method of running the program will be simple, but the precise method depends on how your system has been set up. In addition you will need access to a user manual, tutorial package and any other form of help which is available. It is very unlikely that you will be able to learn to use the DTP program properly without training of some kind. If this training is not given, you are likely to waste many hours.
>
> **2** Find out what printer is available to you to use. With DTP, the printer is critical, since the very precise specifications of text and image size and positions on the paper can only really be dealt with effectively by a laser printer. You will need to set up the DTP software for the correct make and model of printer which will be used before you start creating your first DTP page. Again, if this is not done, much time can be wasted.

As with all current applications software for PCs, there are often two versions available – one for DOS and one for Windows. Pagemaker is one of the most widely used DTP programs, and this one runs under Microsoft Windows.

Desktop publishing features

The basic features of a DTP program are now described:

■ Import text

Text can be prepared first on a word processor, stored as a file on disk, and then loaded into the DTP to appear on the page. The text can then be arranged and manipulated to the user's precise requirements. It is possible to type the text straight onto the DTP screen page, but it is not advisable to do this for large amounts of text, as the editing facilities of the DTP program are not as good as those in a word processor program.

Alternatively, the user may import text from files created elsewhere. For example a user may receive a text file through an electronic mail, and then import this text, or part of it, to the DTP program.

■ Page layout

The prime purpose of the DTP program is to produce a very specific page layout. There are many aspects of the page layout which can be varied, and this is something to which the user should devote time to planning what is needed. This planning is recommended before detailed work on the text and images takes place. The DTP program is not like the word processor program, in that, with a word processor, it is usually easiest to key in the text first, and worry about layout and formatting later. With DTP the opposite is the case.

Once on the page, the text is then formatted into blocks and columns, rather like those in a newspaper or magazine. The number of columns should be specified when the page layout is created, and the user should decide on the size of the gaps between the columns, the lengths of the columns and the size of the top, bottom and side margins. The text may range over one page or a sequence of pages.

■ Images

Pictures may be included on the DTP page. These pictures may be diagrams, digitised photographs (possibly input to the computer from a scanner) or drawings created with other software. The ability of the DTP program to accept (or 'import') files of data from other programs is crucial. There are several standard file formats which are used to store pictures in computer files. These different file formats are recognised by their file name extension; common ones are .BMP (a 'bitmap' file), .PCX (a 'paintbrush' file) and .WMF (a Windows 'metafile').

■ Text fonts

A large number of fonts is generally available to the DTP user. The ability to choose from a wide range of fonts and font sizes is one of the key features of DTP. These fonts should be scalable fonts. This means that once a particular font has been chosen, it is possible to vary the size while still retaining the correct shape of the characters.

Although the same range of fonts may be available in the word processor software, the word processor may not be able to vary their size and position on paper in such a flexible way. For example, with DTP you can change not only the size of the printed characters, but also the space between them and the space between one line and the next.

■ Special effects

Special effects are usually available for text. These effects are intended to add to the appearance of the final document, and so should be used with care. The text effects available may include, for example:

- Transforming text, to change the size and shape of a line of text which is already on the page.
- Changing the angle of text – to create sloping text.
- Varying the angle of individual characters.

■ Image libraries

Libraries of pictures, diagrams symbols and logos can be available on disk, created by the software manufacturers or other PC users, and ready to place on the page of your DTP document.

■ Drawing

The DTP software will include some drawing capabilities. As with the creation of passages of text, it is not recommended that the user create complex drawings in the DTP program itself. It will generally be better to use specialist graphics software and then import the results in the form of a disk file.

Situation

At Sportstown Leisure Centre, some PCs are equipped with DTP software. The large number of leaflets, posters, forms and advertisements which the Leisure Centre produces makes desktop publishing an important time-saving and cost-saving application. When the Leisure Centre first opened in 1989, this whole area of work had to be done by designers and printers external to the centre. This had two main disadvantages: first, there was a considerable delay between recognising the need for a leaflet and getting it back from the printers; secondly, the cost was far higher than with the present DTP system. However, the manager does recognise that when work was sent out the design quality was higher than with the present in-house system. The staff using DTP have improved as they have built up experience with the DTP software, but it is not easy to use, and some training is still required.

Hardware for desktop publishing

The items of hardware which are essential to a typical DTP system are:

- Personal Computer with minimum 286 processor.
- Keyboard.
- Mouse.
- Monitor (this may be a colour or monochrome screen).
- Hard disk drive (capacity 200Mb or more), which is inside the CPU box.
- Floppy disk drive (capacity 720Kb or 1.44Mb), which is at the front of the CPU box.
- Printer capable of printing graphics as well as text.

The list shows a typical hardware specification to run a DTP system. There are, however, many variations to this specification, depending mainly on the requirements for the job.

■ Processor

The PC for a DTP system needs to be quite powerful. This is because of the nature of the processing required. The computer has to be able to process the data received quickly, in order to update the text and images on the screen as the user makes changes to the DTP document. With a less powerful computer, the user would find that, as he or she makes changes via the keyboard or mouse, there is a delay before the effects of those changes are shown on the screen. This is at best annoying, and at worst makes the system unusable for serious DTP work.

For these reasons, a 486 or Pentium processor is ideal, although a 386 processor may be used without any great problem. A processor earlier than the 386 would be impracticable for desktop publishing.

As with word processing, the system should ideally be fully 'WYSIWYG' (what you see is what you get). The whole point of desktop publishing is that the document can be accurately designed on the screen, giving particular attention to layout and typesetting. True WYSIWYG is only possible with a large screen which matches the size of the document you are producing, but, nevertheless, current DTP software does give a reliable indication of the finished document on screen before printing.

■ Monitor

The computer has to store in its memory or on disk the colour of every pixel on the screen, and for a sharp picture a typical monitor with a resolution of 1024×768 pixels represents 750 000 pixels. Each of these pixels may be one of hundreds of different colours. This means that considerable storage space in memory and on disk is required.

■ Disk storage

A hard disk drive is essential to a DTP system. With a networked work station a typical hard disk drive may store from 200Mb to 800Mb. The DTP software will occupy up to 30Mb of this space, and extra space has to be left for the storage of temporary files which are needed whilst documents are in the process of being produced.

Another important factor to consider when a PC is being used for desktop publishing is the speed of the hard disk drive. As was discussed under 'Processors' above, the speed with which the computer is able to make changes on the screen in response to the user's commands is vital. A large part of any delay which exists in this area is the time taken to physically write data onto the hard disk, or to retrieve data from the disk.

The faster the speed of the disk drive, the smaller will be the time taken for this screen updating.

The speed of a hard disk drive is usually measured in milliseconds (ms), and this measurement gives the time for the transfer of a unit of data between the surface of the disk and the RAM memory of the PC.

■ Printer

A printer which can produce high-quality output is essential for a DTP system. There is little point in producing attractive typeset documents on the screen and then outputting to a low quality printer. The only situation where this could be done is where a DTP system is used for the design of the document, and the disk file is taken to an external company for printing, and this is done by some organisations.

Fig. 3 Laser printer for desktop publishing

Because laser printers are relatively expensive to buy (and run), Ian Whicker at the Leisure Centre has asked the staff to use the ink-jets for normal work, and the laser only for final copies of leaflets and other material for the public. This is typical of many office workplaces at present.

▶▶ **FIND OUT**

> Find out whether a laser printer is available to you, what type it is, and what the rules are regarding its use. If you are working on a network, the laser printer may be in a different location to the computer you are working on.

Activity 4.1

SITUATION

Produce an A4 poster for the Wessex Windows annual regional dinner dance.

CONTENTS

Set up a DTP page; enter text and choose appropriate fonts; save file to disk.

Level: INTERMEDIATE

Element: PRESENT INFORMATION

TASKS

1 Run the desktop publisher program.

2 Create a new page with portrait orientation and a single column for text.

3 Enter the following text onto the page:

Wessex Windows

Annual Regional Dinner and Dance

at

The Kings Arms Hotel, Blackdown

Saturday 17 December 1994

8.00 until midnight

Tickets £12.50

4 Select all the text and centre it.

5 Choose a suitable font for all the text, from the range of fonts available on your system.

6 Select the text: 'Annual Regional Dinner and Dance' and make this text large. If necessary, select the rest of the text lines and change the font size to a suitable size.

7 Preview the printout of the document, make any changes necessary to obtain a satisfactory layout, and print the document.

8 Save the file to your own disk or your own user area under the file name DANCE1.

9 Exit the desktop publisher program.

Activity 4.2

SITUATION

Produce an A4 poster to display information on the noticeboard at Sportstown Leisure Centre.

CONTENTS

Set up a DTP page; enter text and choose appropriate fonts; save file to disk.

Level: INTERMEDIATE

Element: PRESENT INFORMATION

TASKS

1 Run the desktop publisher program.

2 Create a new page with portrait orientation and a single column for text.

3 Enter the following text onto the page:

Sportstown Leisure Centre

Annual Membership Subscriptions

are now due.

Please pay at reception

as soon as possible.

Cheques should be made payable to 'Sportstown Direct Leisure'.

4 Select all the text and centre it.

5 Choose a suitable font for all the text, from the range of fonts available on your system.

6 Select the text: 'Annual Membership Subscriptions' and make this text large. If necessary, select the rest of the text lines and change the font size to a suitable size.

7 Preview the printout of the document, make any changes necessary to obtain a satisfactory layout, and print the document.

8 Save the file to your own disk or your own user area under the file name SUBS1.

9 Exit the desktop publisher program.

Activity 4.3

SITUATION

Produce an A4 poster for an advertisement at Sportstown Leisure Centre.

CONTENTS

Set up a DTP page; enter text; select text and apply a range of fonts and font sizes; save and print a DTP page.

Level: INTERMEDIATE

Element: PRESENT INFORMATION

TASKS

1 Run the desktop publisher program.

2 Set up an A4 document (portrait orientation).

3 Key in the data shown below for a leaflet/poster advertising roller discos at Sportstown Leisure Centre.

> Sportstown Leisure Centre
>
> Roller Disco
>
> Every Saturday evening
>
> The best roller surface
>
> plus the best disco in town
>
> 14-year-olds and upwards
>
> Cost: only £1.75

4 Select all the text and choose a suitable font from a range of fonts. Centre all the text in the document.

5 Select 'Sportstown Leisure Centre' and embolden the text.

6 Select 'Roller Disco'. Embolden the text and change the font size to a large size.

7 Select 'The best roller surface plus the best disco in town'. Embolden and italicise the text.

8 Study the layout of the page. If necessary, insert (or delete) new line characters so that the text fills the page and looks balanced. To insert a new line character, put the software into text edit mode, move the cursor to the start of the line, then press the **<Enter>** key. To remove a new line character, put the software into text edit mode, move the cursor to the start of the line, then press the **<Backspace>** key.

The document should resemble the example shown in Fig. 4, but you may use different fonts, sizes and spacing.

9 Save the document to your own disk or your own user area under the file name DISCO1. Make a back-up file using a suitable name to another disk or user area.

10 Print the document.

11 Exit the DTP program.

Activity 4.4

SITUATION

Produce an A4 poster for an advertisement at Sportstown Leisure Centre.

CONTENTS

Set up a DTP page; enter text; select text and apply a range of fonts and font sizes; save and print a DTP page.

Level: INTERMEDIATE

Element: PRESENT INFORMATION

TASKS

1 Run the desktop publisher program.

2 Set up an A4 document (portrait orientation).

Sportstown Leisure Centre

Roller Disco

Every Saturday evening
6.30 - 9.30

The best roller surface plus the best disco in town

14-year-olds and upwards
Cost: only £1.75

Fig. 4

3 Key in the data shown below for an exhibition basketball match to be held at Sportstown Leisure Centre.

Sportstown Leisure Centre

Exhibition Basketball Match

Friday 21 January 1994

7.15pm–9.15pm

Sportstown Eagles

play

Bricknall Pirates

plus entertainments

Entry ticket in advance only – £5.75

4 Select all the text and choose a suitable font from a range of fonts. Centre all the text in the document.

5 Select 'Sportstown Leisure Centre' and embolden the text.

6 Select 'Exhibition Basketball Match'. Embolden the text and change the font size to a large size.

7 Select 'Sportstown Eagles play Bricknall Pirates'. Embolden and italicise the text.

8 Study the layout of the page. If necessary, insert (or delete) new line characters so that the text fills the page and looks balanced. The document should resemble the example shown in Fig. 5, but you may use different fonts, sizes and spacing.

9 Save the document to your own disk or your own user area under the file name BBALL1. Make a back-up file using a suitable name to another disk or user area.

10 Print the document.

11 Exit the DTP program.

Sportstown Leisure Centre

Exhibition Basketball Match

Friday 21 January 1994
7.15 - 9.15 pm

*Sportstown Eagles
play
Bricknall Pirates*

plus entertainments

Entry by ticket in advance only - £5.75

Fig. 5

Activity 4.5

SITUATION

Produce an A4 leaflet to advertise a conference for leisure centre managers.

CONTENTS

Use a word processor to prepare, check and store text in suitable format for export to DTP program. Set up DTP page, import text and change the text to achieve suitable layout. Save and print document.

Level: INTERMEDIATE, ADVANCED

Elements: PREPARE, PROCESS, PRESENT INFORMATION

TASKS

1 Run the word processor on your system.

2 Enter the following text to the word processor, all left justified:

Conference

The Implications for Centre Managers of Information Technology in Leisure Centres

Venue: New Trade Hall, Salisbury, Wiltshire

Date: Saturday September 16 (10.30–4.30)

Sunday September 17 (9.00–2.00) 1994

Saturday:

10.30–11.00	Coffee and welcome
11.00–12.30	Computerised activity booking and accounts systems
12.30–2.00	Lunch
2.00–4.30	Computer analysis of activity usage

Sunday:

9.00–11.00	Implications for jobs and retraining
11.00–11.15	Break

Desktop publishing   73

```
11.15–12.00    Workshops on training videos
12.00–1.00     Lunch
1.00–2.00      Plenary session
```

Open to all current and potential centre managers.

Applications to Education Dept., Leisure Management Head Office.

3 Save the file to your own disk or your own user area under the file name CONF1. Make a backup file to disk (under a different file name) in case of accidental loss.

4 Exit the word processor program.

5 Run the desktop publisher program on your system.

6 Create a new file for a portrait A4 document with single column layout.

7 Import the CONF1 file to the DTP document and place it on the page.

8 Select the text and choose suitable font styles and sizes to produce an attractively laid out document which can be sent to Leisure Centre managers and displayed on notice boards.

9 Select the first six lines of the text, and centre the text on those lines. In the same way, centre the text from 'Open to all . . .' onwards.

10 Save the file to your own disk or your own user area under the file name CONF2. Also make a back-up copy of the file under a different name.

11 Preview the printout, in both landscape and portrait modes. Select the most appropriate mode. Make any adjustments which are necessary, and print the final version. In your own handwriting, neatly label the changes you have made from the first (word processed) version of the document. Also explain briefly on the printout why you have chosen either landscape or portrait.

12 List on screen, and then print on paper, the files in the current directory, including the file names for this activity.

13 Exit the DTP program.

Activity 4.6

SITUATION

Use DTP to produce a document for Sportstown Leisure Centre.

CONTENTS

Produce a word processor document; check the text for accuracy; save in suitable format for export to DTP. Set up a DTP page; import word processor document and make necessary adjustments to the layout; use lines/boxes in DTP; print a document.

Level: ADVANCED

Elements: PREPARE, PROCESS, PRESENT INFORMATION

TASKS

1 Run the word processor program and key in the text below. The text is for a leaflet which advertises children's parties at the Sportstown Leisure Centre. This text is to be stored as a file and then loaded into the DTP program, so do not include any special character or paragraph formatting at this stage.

Children's parties

If your child has a birthday soon, why not hold the party at Sportstown Leisure Centre?

We have all the facilities you need, and an enthusiastic staff who are guaranteed to make your party a success.

Food can be laid on, with party hats, novelties and games.

The party lasts 2 hours, and can start any time between 12noon and 4pm on Saturday or Sunday.

To book your party, fill in the slip below, and hand it in to reception, where the staff on duty will discuss your detailed requirements with you.

The cost is from £5 per guest.

2 Use the spelling checker and a visual, on-screen check to verify the accuracy of your data entry. Correct any mistakes.

3 Save the file to your own disk or your own user area under the file name PARTYTXT. Depending upon the particular word processor and DTP software which you are using on your system, the file may need to be saved in a special format to allow it to be imported to a DTP document. Ensure that you save in the correct file format. (Refer to your user manual or lecturer for guidance.)

4 Print the text and keep the printout for reference.

5 Exit the word processor program.

6 Run the DTP program.

7 Set up a single page document for A4 paper (or nearest on your system) with two text columns. Switch on the ruler, so that the objects on the page can be accurately aligned.

8 Import the text file called PARTYTXT which you previously created as a word processor file and place it on the page. Arrange the text in the two columns on the page, allowing sufficient space at the bottom of the page for the return slip. Select the heading 'Children's parties', choose a suitable font and font size from the range of available fonts and embolden and italicise the text. Select all the rest of the text and choose a suitable font and font size for this text.

9 Across the bottom of the page (in a single column), place the text shown below for a return slip.

Please arrange a party for (NAME): _____

To be held on: _____ **Tel no:** _____

Time to start the party: _____

Number of guests: _____ **Price to pay:** _____

The spaces where customers fill in the details may be solid lines (as above), dotted lines or boxes.

10 Surround the return slip text by a box, using the box drawing or line-drawing facility of the DTP program.

11 Examine the document and make any amendments necessary to obtain a neat, clear and well-balanced layout.

12 Switch off the ruler feature. Also change any other system options (such as measurement units or printer drivers) back to their initial position for the benefit of other users of the system.

13 Save the file to your own disk or your own user area under the file name PARTY1. Also make a back-up copy of the file under a different file name.

14 Preview the printout of the document, make any adjustments which are necessary, and print the final version. In your own handwriting, neatly label the changes you have made from the first (word-processed) version of the document.

15 List on screen, and then print on paper, the files in the current directory, including the file names for this activity.

16 Exit the DTP program.

Activity 4.7

SITUATION

Use DTP to produce a document for Sportstown Leisure Centre.

CONTENTS

Produce a word processor document; check the text for accuracy; save in suitable format for export to DTP; set up a DTP page; import word processor document and make necessary adjustments to the layout; use lines/boxes in DTP; print a document.

Level: ADVANCED

Elements: PREPARE, PROCESS, PRESENT INFORMATION

TASKS

1 Run the word processor program and key in the text below. The text is for a leaflet which advertises the Sportstown Leisure Centre running club. This text is to be stored as a file and then loaded into the DTP program, so do not include any special character or paragraph formatting at this stage.

Sportstown Runners

Our new Athletics Arena, adjacent to the centre, has an excellent all-weather track on which to train.

Runners should think about using the Sportstown track for these reasons:

- Easier on the feet than road running, leading to fewer injuries.
- Train with other runners for companionship and competition.
- Safer than road running, especially in darkness hours.

The track may be used on a casual basis at £2.75 per 2-hour session (any time during the week), or you may prefer to buy a season ticket for £25 per year. This entitles you to use the track any time it is open, all year round.

For more information, fill in the slip below, and hand it in to reception.

2 Use the spell checker and a visual, on-screen check to verify the accuracy of your data entry. Correct any mistakes.

3 Save the file to your own disk or your own user area under the file name RUNTXT. Depending upon the particular word processor and DTP software which you are using on your system, the file may need to be saved in a special format to allow it to be imported to a DTP document. Ensure that you save in the correct file format. (Refer to your user manual or lecturer for guidance.)

4 Print the text and keep the printout for reference.

5 Exit the word processor program.

6 Run the DTP program.

7 Set up a single-page document for A4 paper (or nearest on your system) with two text columns.

8 Import the text file called RUNTXT which you previously created as a word processor file and place it on the page. Arrange the text in the two columns on the page, allowing sufficient space at the bottom of

the page for the return slip. Select the heading 'Sportstown Runners', choose a suitable font and font size from the range of available fonts and embolden and italicise the text. Select all the rest of the text and choose a suitable font and font size for this text.

9 Across the bottom of the page, place the text shown below for a return slip.

Please send me more information on using the new Sportstown Athletics Arena running track. I am interested in:

- Joining Sportstown Runners   _____
- Using the track on a casual basis   _____
- Making use of a season ticket   _____

Name: _____

Address: _____

                                   _____

                                   _____

Telephone no: _____

The spaces where customers fill in the details may be solid lines (as above), dotted lines or boxes.

10 Surround the return slip text by a box, using the box-drawing or line-drawing facility of the DTP program.

11 Examine the document and make any amendments necessary to obtain a neat, clear and well-balanced layout.

12 Save the file to your own disk or your own user area under the file name RUNNER1. Also make a back-up copy of the file under a different file name.

13 Preview the printout of the document, make any adjustments which are necessary, and print the final version. In your own handwriting, neatly label the changes you have made from the first (word-processed) version of the document. Also explain on the printout

what adjustments you made to the appearance of the document in order to obtain a neat, clear and well-balanced layout.

14 List on screen, and then print on paper, the files in the current directory, including the file names for this activity.

15 Exit the DTP program.

5 Spreadsheet

Background to spreadsheet

The spreadsheet is a very powerful application for computers of all types: mainframes, mid-range and PCs. It is used extensively in businesses, often for financial purposes. Popular PC programs include:

- Excel
- Supercalc
- Lotus 1-2-3
- Borland's Quattro

Example applications

Some example uses of the spreadsheet in business are as follows:

■ Petty cash recording and totalling

A spreadsheet model is created which will allow the user to enter petty cash amounts for each day of the week or month. (Petty cash is small amounts of cash which have been spent on day-to-day expenses.) These amounts are entered with a code into a particular column, according to what types of things the amounts have been spent on. For example, there may be columns for postage, travel fares, stationery and refreshments.

The job of the spreadsheet is to add up the amounts as they occur

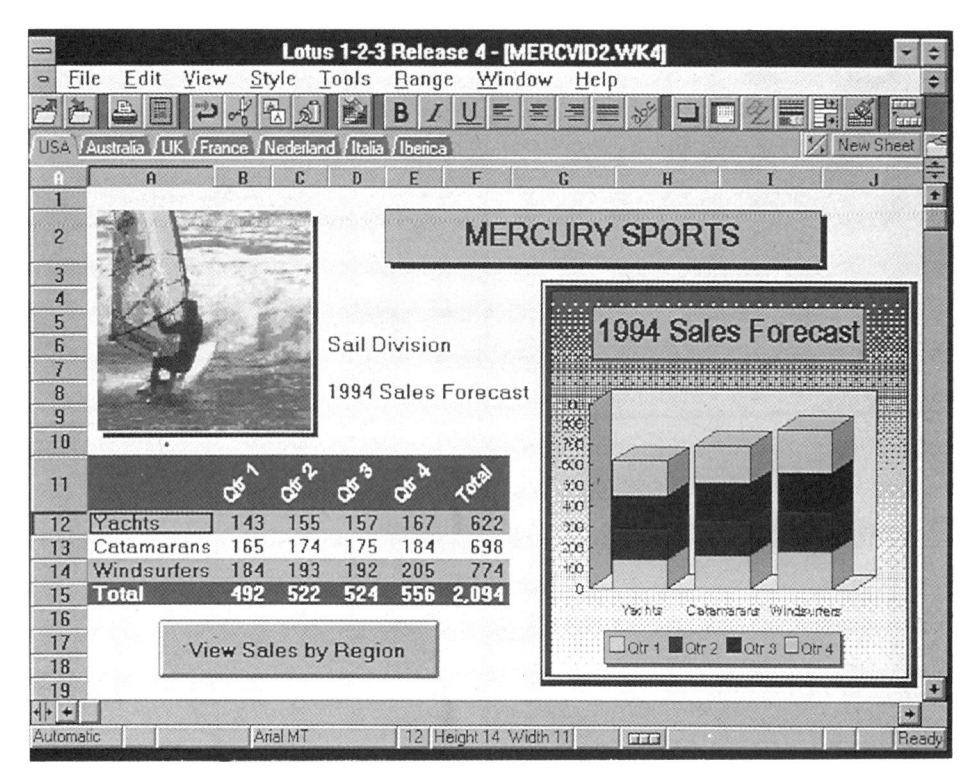

Fig. 6 Spreadsheet display

throughout the week or month. At any time, by referring to the spreadsheet, the user can see how much petty cash has been spent so far, and also what categories it has been spent on. It is the formulae in the spreadsheet model which do the calculations, saving the user time.

■ VAT calculations

Spreadsheet models may be set up to carry out various VAT calculations. Again, the formulae, once set up in the model and saved to disk, save the user considerable time. Amounts are entered and the spreadsheet quickly calculates the VAT on each item, together with totals if required.

■ Cash flow forecasting

When a new business venture is being planned, or even when an existing business operation needs planning, a cash flow forecast may be developed on a computer spreadsheet. Expected amounts of income and expenditure are entered for each month, usually over a six-month or twelve-month period. The formulae which are placed in the spreadsheet carry out an automatic totalling of all the items for both income and expenditure for each month. Allowing for a starting cash balance, the end of month cash balance can now be shown for each month of the period. The spreadsheet, if set up correctly, will carry forward the closing balance at the end of one month, to become the opening balance at the start of the next month.

A typical layout of the cash flow forecast is as follows:

	JAN	FEB	MAR	APR	MAY	JUN
OPENING BALANCE						
INCOME						
Cash sales						
Credit sales						
Other income						
TOTAL INCOME						
EXPENDITURE						
Wages						
Rent						
Stock						
Electricity						
Loan interest						
Advertising						
Other expenditure						
TOTAL EXPENDITURE						
MONTHLY SURPLUS						
CLOSING BALANCE						

The cash flow forecast spreadsheet may then used in an experimental way. Since the figures entered are estimates only, they cannot be absolutely fixed. Therefore, the figures can be varied, and the user can see what the cash position would be for different sets of estimated figures. For example, one can ask the question 'What would the bank balance be for each month of the year if the sales figures are £10 000 higher each month?' The changes are made to the sales figures (by simply overtyping the numbers in the cells of the spreadsheet), and the spreadsheet immediately shows the changed bank balance. If this were done manually, it would be a lengthy process.

■ Projection of future sales from past records

Forecasts are a common business requirement, and there are various ways in which forecasts may be made. Most rely on records of past information, such as sales of the business over the past two years. This information may be entered on the spreadsheet together with formulae to make the calculations which will produce the forecast. Of course, the actual forecasts made are only as good as the accuracy of the information which is fed in, and the suitability of the method of arriving at the forecast.

■ Setting and keeping records of budget expenditures

The spreadsheet can be used as a planning tool, but also as a tool for monitoring and recording information. An example is the setting of expenditure budgets, to plan how a total amount of money will be spent over the coming year. The plan can be made on the spreadsheet, and then, when expenditure actually takes place it is recorded on the spreadsheet. Using the correct formulae, the spreadsheet will compare planned spending to what has actually been spent (for a number of different categories), and the budget variances can be shown. (The budget variance is the difference between the budgeted and the actual figure.)

■ Statistical analysis of numerical information

Most spreadsheets can be used for a large number of statistical tasks. There are statistical functions which can be included in formulae, to calculate, for example, the average of a set of values in a list, or the maximum or minimum value in a list. In this way, sets of data can be entered in the rows and columns of the spreadsheet, and the spreadsheet will calculate the required statistics.

In addition, spreadsheets are used to create graphs and charts of numerical information. Generally this is done by highlighting or selecting particular rows and columns of the sheets, and giving the command to draw a specific type of graph. An advantage here over other methods of drawing graphs is that, once the graphs have been set up on the spreadsheet, if the user changes the figures, the graphs will change automatically.

The structure of a spreadsheet

The spreadsheet display itself resembles a very large sheet of paper which has been ruled into rows and columns. Each cell in the spreadsheet has a cell reference, such as B3, which would mean column B, row 3. This arrangement produces thousands of boxes or cells, into which information can be placed. Although it is unusual to use more than a hundred or so cells of the spreadsheet, it is possible to work with extremely large sheets. The only problem with large sheets is that the (RAM) memory of the computer is quickly filled up by spreadsheet data.

The size of a computer's screen is obviously limited, and so it is possible to move around the spreadsheet by pressing the cursor control keys or by moving the mouse. The rows and columns of the spreadsheet will scroll, so that the screen of the computer acts like a window on a much larger sheet.

The number of cells which can be used depends in part on the memory size of the computer. Some areas of the spreadsheet may be automatically stored on disk as they move off the edge of the screen, but this tends to slow down movement around the spreadsheet, which can make it awkward to use. If the user intends to develop and work with very large spreadsheets it is best to install extra memory modules to increase the size of the computer's RAM.

There are three kinds of information which can be placed in a cell of the spreadsheet:

1 A number.
2 Some text.
3 A formula.

■ Numbers

A number can be put into a cell of the spreadsheet. The number can be stored and displayed in one of many different formats, for example:

- money in pounds and pence;
- a percentage;
- a number rounded to a fixed number of decimal places;
- a number in 'floating decimal point' format (similar to the method of display of numbers on a calculator).

Normally the format required for cells containing numbers is set as a separate operation from the actual entry of the number itself into the cell.

For example, to store £32.00 in a spreadsheet cell, the user would just type in the number 32 and press the **<Enter>** key. Then an instruction can be given to display the number in money format, showing both decimal places for the pence. This could be done individually, one cell at a time, but it is more usual to decide which areas of the spreadsheet are to contain money values, select or highlight those areas of the sheet, and then give the instruction to display all these amounts in money format. This operation can be done either before or after the actual entry of the numbers.

Numbers are usually right justified. This means that when you type in a number it will appear on the right-hand side of the cell width. This is normal, since if you wrote down a series of figures for adding up on paper, you would need to right justify them so that the units were under units, tens were under tens, and so on.

■ Text

Text is dealt with in a similar way to numbers; the text is placed in the cells and the format is specified. This format may be to centre the text within the width of the cell, or to align it to the left or right of the cell. Text may overflow into other cells as long as the cells it overflows into are left blank. This feature is used for placing headings and other text labels on the spreadsheet.

In addition, most spreadsheet programs will allow the user to specify the font to be used when printing the spreadsheet data on paper. You may wish to embolden, underline or italicise the text (or some of it), and this should be possible.

■ Formulae

A formula can be placed into any cell of the spreadsheet that does not contain any other information. By setting up formulae the user is really programming the computer to carry out a series of calculations.

A formula is an instruction which tells the computer to combine the numbers in other cells together in some way; for example, to add a column of figures and to place the answer in that cell.

The formula gives the computer a precise calculation to carry out. The calculation can include a wide range of arithmetical, statistical or scientific calculations, depending upon the spreadsheet program being used. For example, Lotus 1-2-3 includes a large number of pre-set statistical functions which can be included in a formula.

■ Recalculation

Recalculation is the feature which gives the spreadsheet its power. The fact that you can place a formula in a cell means that the computer can automatically carry out calculations whenever the numbers in the spreadsheet change. The spreadsheet is useful, therefore, when investigating financial possibilities, such as setting budgets or costing projects. The recalculation is done very quickly, due to the speed of operation of the CPU, and so hundreds of cells in a spreadsheet will take only a fraction of a second to recalculate.

■ Copying the contents of cells

When putting data into a spreadsheet, the user often has to repeat the same data for a number of different cells. There is no need to retype the same information over and over again. The copy or replicate feature allows you to highlight a range of cells and copy the contents to another range of cells. This saves a lot of time, and it even works when copying formulae. The computer will automatically adjust the cell references in the formulae, so that, for example, the formula to add the total of one column can be copied across to do the same in another column.

■ Draw graphs of data in the spreadsheet

This is a feature of all current spreadsheet programs. The reason it is there is that, once calculations have been carried out in the spreadsheet, there is often a need to present or communicate the results to other people. The best way to do this may be in the form of a table, in which case a part of the spreadsheet may simply be printed out, or it might be better to present the results in the form of a graph.

The types of graphs offered will usually be pie chart, line chart, bar chart (simple or compound), scatter diagram, or a mixture of these. The method of drawing the chart is generally to select or highlight the row(s) or column(s) of figures to be charted and then to give the command to chart them. The software will do any calculations necessary, such as working out the scale to use on the axes of the chart or working out the sizes of the slices of pie in a pie chart.

Activity 5.1

SITUATION

Set up a spreadsheet model for totalling takings for drinks at Sportstown Leisure Centre.

CONTENTS

Set up spreadsheet model with simple formulae; enter data; save file to disk; make adjustments to fit printout on paper; include spreadsheet data in a report.

Level: INTERMEDIATE

Elements: PREPARE, PROCESS INFORMATION

TASKS

1 Run the spreadsheet program.

2 Create a new spreadsheet and enter the following data for drinks sold at Sportstown Leisure Centre. The function of the spreadsheet is to automatically calculate the money taken when the number of drinks sold is entered.

	Price (pence)	Number sold	TOTAL (£)
Tea	40	140	
Coffee	55	127	
Lemonade	60	38	
Cola	50	45	
Fruit juice	45	24	
TOTAL			

3 Right-align the three column headings so that they are vertically in line with the numbers.

4 If the names of the drinks are not left-aligned, select or highlight them and make them left-aligned.

5 Place a formula in the 'TOTAL' column in the row for 'Tea' to perform the calculation:

(Price × Number sold)/100

in order to calculate the total money taken for each type of drink.

6 Copy the formula down the column for all the other drinks.

7 Place a formula at the foot of the 'Number sold' column in the 'TOTAL' row to calculate the total number of drinks (of all types) sold. Copy this formula across to the 'TOTAL' column to obtain a grand total for money taken.

8 Save the spreadsheet to your own disk or your own user area under the file name DRINKS1.

9 Preview the printout of the spreadsheet, and, after making any necessary adjustments to the font or the column widths in order to fit the printout onto one sheet of paper, print the spreadsheet.

10 Insert an extra row immediately below the 'Fruit juice' row for 'Milk,' which was omitted in error. Enter the price of milk drinks, which was 40p, and the number sold, which was 36.

11 Place the required formulae in the 'Milk' row in order to calculate the money taken for milk drinks.

12 Check the formulae on the total row. If they do not include the extra row, change the formulae.

13 Save the new version under the file name (overwriting the previous file). Also make a back-up copy of the file under a different file name.

14 Print the final version of the spreadsheet. In your own handwriting, neatly label one column of figures, to show that the numbers have been right-aligned.

15 List on screen, and then print on paper, the files in the current directory, including the file names for this activity.

16 Exit the spreadsheet program.

17 You must now include your spreadsheet results in a short report. Use a word processor program to prepare the heading and introduction for this report. The introduction should state the function of the spreadsheet and briefly how the results are worked out.

18 Use cut and paste (or a similar technique, depending on the software you are using), to transfer the spreadsheet results to the report. You may need to make adjustments to the layout in order to fit the results appropriately on the page. Add your own short commentary, describing briefly what the results show.

19 Save the report, preview and then obtain a printout.

20 Exit the word processor program.

Activity 5.2

SITUATION

Set up a spreadsheet for points calculations in a 5-a-side football competition.

CONTENTS

Set up spreadsheet model with simple formulae; enter data; save file to disk; make adjustments to fit printout on paper; include spreadsheet data in a report.

Level: INTERMEDIATE

Elements: PREPARE, PROCESS, PRESENT INFORMATION

TASKS

1 Run the spreadsheet program.

2 Create a new spreadsheet and enter the following data for games won and drawn in the Sportstown Leisure Centre's 5-a-side football tournament. The function of the spreadsheet is to automatically calculate the points scored when the results are entered. The number of points scored are three for a win and one point for a draw.

	Games won	Games drawn	Points scored
Tigers	4	2	
Wolves	3	1	
Cubs	5	0	
Roosters	1	3	
Stallions	6	1	
TOTAL			

3 Right-align the three column headings so that they are vertically in line with the numbers.

4 If the names of the teams are not left-aligned, select or highlight them and make them left-aligned.

5 Place a formula in the 'Points scored' column in the row for 'Tigers' to perform the calculation:

(games won × 3) + (games drawn)

in order to calculate the total points scored for each football team.

6 Copy the formula down the column for all the other teams.

7 Place a formula at the foot of the Points scored column to add up the points scored by all the teams together.

8 Save the spreadsheet to your own disk or your own user area under the file name FBALL1.

9 Preview the printout of the spreadsheet, and, after making any necessary adjustments to the font or the column widths in order to fit the printout onto one sheet of paper, print the spreadsheet.

10 Insert an extra row immediately below the 'Stallions' row for another team, called 'Badgers', which was omitted in error. Enter the 'Games won' which was 3 and the 'Games drawn' which was 4.

11 Place the required formula in the 'Badgers' row in order to calculate the points scored for this team.

12 Check the formula on the total row. If it does not include the extra row, change the formula.

13 Save the new version under the same file name (overwriting the previous file). Also make a back-up copy of the file under a different file name.

14 Print the final version of the spreadsheet. In your own handwriting, neatly label one column of figures, to show that the numbers have been right-aligned.

15 List on screen, and then print on paper, the files in the current directory, including the file names for this activity.

16 Exit the spreadsheet program.

17 You must now include your spreadsheet results in a short report. Use a word processor program to prepare the heading and introduction for this report. The introduction should state the function of the spreadsheet and briefly how the results are worked out.

18 Use cut and paste (or a similar technique, depending on the software you are using), to transfer the spreadsheet results to the report. You may need to make adjustments to the layout in order to fit the results appropriately on the page. Add your own short commentary, describing briefly what the results show.

19 Save the report, preview and then obtain a printout.

20 Exit the word processor program.

Activity 5.3

SITUATION

Set up a spreadsheet for the monthly sales analysis of Wessex Windows.

CONTENTS

Set up spreadsheet model with simple formulae; enter data; save file to disk; make adjustments to fit printout on paper; include spreadsheet data in a report.

Level: INTERMEDIATE

Elements: PREPARE, PROCESS, PRESENT INFORMATION

TASKS

1 Run the spreadsheet program.

2 Place the heading **Monthly sales analysis** at the top of the spreadsheet. Starting in the second column, enter the following headings, right-aligned:

| UPVC WINDOWS | UPVC DOORS | HARDWOOD WINDOWS | HARDWOOD DOORS |

3 In the first column, on the next row after the headings, enter the following salesperson names, left-aligned:

Jones
Smith
Mallow
Phillips
Williams

4 Enter the amount for each salesperson as shown in the table below:

	UPVC WINDOWS	UPVC DOORS	HARDWOOD WINDOWS	HARDWOOD DOORS
Jones	1240	800	3540	1270
Smith	2750	2060	5400	1340
Mallow	2200	1000	5500	1520
Phillips	1090	1050	2300	1100
Williams	990	500	6090	1300

5 Save the spreadsheet to your own disk or your own user area under the file name TEAMSALE.

6 Preview the printout of the spreadsheet, make any corrections necessary to fit the spreadsheet on the paper you are using, and print the spreadsheet.

7 Some errors have been found in the figures. Make the following corrections:

Smith's UPVC WINDOWS sales should be 2570.

Phillips's HARDWOOD WINDOWS sales should be 4090.

Herbert has recently joined the team, and his sales must now be included in the figures (immediately underneath the others):

	UPVC WINDOWS	UPVC DOORS	HARDWOOD WINDOWS	HARDWOOD DOORS
Herbert	2070	190	200	1050

8 Save the spreadsheet under the same file name, overwriting the previous version.

9 Place a formula at the foot of the first column which shows sales figures to add the total for all the team members. Copy this formula across the same row of the spreadsheet to the other columns.

10 Place the heading 'TOTAL' immediately to the right of the 'HARDWOOD DOORS' heading.

11 Place a formula under this heading to find the total sales for each team member; then copy this formula downwards to find the totals for all the other members of the sales team.

12 Save the new version under the same file name (overwriting the previous file). Also make a back-up copy of the file under a different file name.

13 Print the final version of the spreadsheet. In your own handwriting, neatly label one column of figures, to show that the numbers have been right-aligned.

14 List on screen, and then print on paper, the files in the current directory, including the file names for this activity.

15 Exit the spreadsheet program.

16 You must now include your spreadsheet results in a short report. Use a word processor program to prepare the heading and introduction for this report. The introduction should state the function of the spreadsheet and briefly how the results are worked out.

17 Use cut and paste (or a similar technique, depending on the software you are using), to transfer the spreadsheet results to the report. You may need to make adjustments to the layout in order to fit the results appropriately on the page. Add your own short commentary, describing briefly what the results show.

18 Save the report, preview and then obtain a printout.

19 Exit the word processor program.

Activity 5.4

SITUATION

Set up a spreadsheet to make wages calculations.

CONTENTS

Set up spreadsheet model with simple formulae; enter data; save file to disk; make adjustments to fit printout on paper; include spreadsheet data in a report.

Levels: INTERMEDIATE, ADVANCED

Elements: PREPARE, PROCESS INFORMATION

TASKS

1 Run the spreadsheet program.

2 Set up a spreadsheet model to calculate the wages of employees whose details are shown in the table below. (If desired you may use the same layout in your spreadsheet model, but this is not essential.)

	Rate per hour (£)	Hours this week	Wages (£)	Trade Union deduction (1%)
J Smith	7.50	40		
F Bloggs	12.00	32		
J Jones	5.75	34		
H Higgins	5.75	34		
B Briggs	5.75	36		
S Simple	4.00	37		
V Granger	5.75	38		
J Moran	2.50	46		

3 Put a formula in the 'Wages' column to calculate the wages for J Smith (rate per hour multiplied by hours this week). Copy this formula down to the other rows to obtain the wages for all the other employees.

4 Put formulae at the foot of the 'Hours this week' and 'Wages' columns to find the totals for all employees.

5 Save the spreadsheet. Ensure that the column headings are right-aligned (to match the numbers in those columns) and set all the numbers to display with the correct number of decimal places (two decimal places for money, and no decimal places for hours worked).

6 Ensure that the spreadsheet will print on one A4 sheet of paper. To do this, you may have to change the column width for some columns, or change the font size. If your spreadsheet program allows, preview the printout on screen before sending it to the printer.

7 Put a formula in the Trade Union deduction column to calculate 1% of

the wages for each employee, and total this column at its foot.

8 Save the new version under the same file name (overwriting the previous file). Also make a back-up copy of the file under a different file name.

9 Print the final version of the spreadsheet. In your own handwriting, neatly label two spreadsheet cells, one which has been right-aligned, and the other which has been set to display two decimal places.

10 Print the spreadsheet formulae so that your lecturer may check that you are using appropriate formulae. When printing the spreadsheet formulae, the layout is not important, so do not make any adjustments to the layout at this stage.

11 List on screen, and then print on paper, the files in the current directory, including the file names for this activity.

12 Exit the spreadsheet program.

13 You must now include your spreadsheet results in a short report. Use a word processor program to prepare the heading and introduction for this report. The introduction should state the function of the spreadsheet and briefly how the results are worked out.

14 Use cut and paste (or a similar technique, depending on the software you are using), to transfer the spreadsheet results to the report. You may need to make adjustments to the layout in order to fit the results appropriately on the page. Add your own short commentary, describing briefly what the results show.

15 Save the report, preview and then obtain a printout.

16 Exit the word processor program.

Activity 5.5

SITUATION

Set up a spreadsheet model to make consultancy fee calculations.

CONTENTS

Set up spreadsheet model with simple formulae; enter data; save file to disk; include spreadsheet data in a report.

Levels: INTERMEDIATE, ADVANCED

Elements: PREPARE, PROCESS, PRESENT INFORMATION

TASKS

1 Run the spreadsheet program.

2 Set up a spreadsheet model to calculate invoice amounts for consultancy fees which are payable by customers whose details are shown below. (If desired you may use the same layout in your spreadsheet model, but this is not essential.)

	Consultancy hours to date	Rate per hour	Fees due	VAT (17.5%)	Total due
Smith & Co.	23	24.00			
Higgins Ltd	17	24.00			
Stone & son	9	24.00			
Pete's Pizza Pad	21	17.50			
Abbey investments	12	24.00			
Spire fundholdings	10	27.00			
James James & Jones	48	24.00			
Tech-compleat plc	23	17.50			

3 Lock the spreadsheet cells containing text, to guard against accidental overtyping. Put a formula in the 'Fees due' column to calculate the fees for Smith & Co. (consultancy hours to date multiplied by rate per hour). Copy this formula down to the other rows to obtain the fees due for all the other customers.

4 Put formulae at the foot of the 'Consultancy hours to date' and 'Fees due' columns to find the totals for all customers.

5 Save the spreadsheet. Ensure that the column headings are right-aligned (to match the numbers in those columns) and set all the numbers to display with the correct number of decimal places (two decimal places for money, and no decimal places for hours).

6 Ensure that the spreadsheet will print on one A4 sheet of paper. To do

this, you may have to change the column width for some columns, or change the font size. If your spreadsheet program allows, preview the printout on screen before sending it to the printer.

7 Put a formula in the VAT (17.5%) column to calculate 17.5% of the fees for each customer, and total this column at its foot. Enter suitable formulae in the 'Total due' column.

8 Save the new version under the same file name (overwriting the previous file). Also make a back-up copy of the file under a different file name.

9 Print the final version of the spreadsheet. In your own handwriting, neatly label two spreadsheet cells, one which has been right-aligned, and the other which has been set to display two decimal places.

10 Print the spreadsheet formulae so that your lecturer may check that you are using appropriate formulae. When printing the spreadsheet formulae, the layout is not important, so do not make any adjustments to the layout at this stage.

11 List on screen, and then print on paper, the files in the current directory, including the file names for this activity.

12 Exit the spreadsheet program.

13 You must now include your spreadsheet results in a short report. Use a word processor program to prepare the heading and introduction for this report. The introduction should state the function of the spreadsheet and briefly how the results are worked out.

14 Use cut and paste (or a similar technique, depending on the software you are using), to transfer the spreadsheet results to the report. You may need to make adjustments to the layout in order to fit the results appropriately on the page. Add your own short commentary, describing briefly what the results show.

15 Save the report, preview and then obtain a printout.

16 Exit the word processor program.

Activity 5.6

SITUATION

Set up a spreadsheet model to make calculations for an invoice.

CONTENTS

Create spreadsheet model with simple formulae; save to disk and make adjustments to fit printout to paper; include spreadsheet results in a report.

Levels: INTERMEDIATE, ADVANCED

Elements: PREPARE, PROCESS, PRESENT INFORMATION

TASKS

1 Run the spreadsheet program.

2 Set up a spreadsheet model with the layout shown in order to produce an invoice for the details given below. Note that you will need to change the width of the first column of the spreadsheet in order to fit in the item details.

Customer's name and address:
F Dickinson
28 Larch Drive
READING
Berks
RG13 5TY

Item	Price (£)	Delivery (£)	VAT (£)	Item total (£)
Toshiba Tl850 386SX 80Mb + Windows 3.1 & Mouse	1470			
Toshiba Tl850C 386SX 120Mb + Windows 3.1 & Mouse	1549			
Canon BJ10SX Printer	1299			
Taxan 789LR VGA monitor 1024 × 768 dots (non-interlaced)	299			

3 Place a formula at the bottom of the 'Price' column to calculate the total price for the customer.

4 The delivery is £7.50 on each item. Place the amount £7.50 in the 'Delivery' column for each item.

5 VAT is charged at the rate of 17.5% on all items. This charge is based on the price plus the delivery charge. Place a formula in the 'VAT' column for the first item to calculate:

(price + delivery) × 17.5%.

When you have verified that this calculates the correct VAT amount, use the spreadsheet's copy function to copy the formula to the other items.

6 Place a formula in the 'Item total' column for the first item to calculate:

price + delivery + VAT.

Use the spreadsheet's copy function to copy this formula to the other items.

7 Save the file to your own disk or your own user area under the file name INVOICE1.

8 Check the alignment of the headings and the data for the 'Price', 'Delivery', 'VAT' and 'Item total' columns; make all the information in these columns right-aligned.

9 Preview the printout and, if necessary, change the font size to make the spreadsheet print on one A4 sheet of paper. Print the spreadsheet.

10 Erase the data in the spreadsheet, but keep the layout and the formulae, and save under the name INVOICE (as a template).

11 Now complete and print a second invoice, with the details which follow:

Customer's name & address:
H Higginbottom Information Services
Cliff Cottage
Sea View Road
Dover
Kent
DV10 7HG

Item	Price (£)	Delivery (£)	VAT (£)	Item total (£)
Hercules Graphite Windows accelerator card	259			
Aries FAXIT Pocket Fax/modem	158			

12 Preview the printout. Make any changes necessary to fit the spreadsheet onto one sheet of A4 paper. Print the spreadsheet.

13 Save the spreadsheet to your own disk or your own user area under the file name INVOICE2. Also make a back-up copy of the file under a different file name and on a different drive or directory.

14 Print the final version of the spreadsheet. In your own handwriting, neatly label one column of figures, to show that the numbers have been right-aligned.

15 List on screen, and then print on paper, the files in the current directory, including the file names for this activity.

16 Exit the spreadsheet program.

17 You must now include your latest spreadsheet results in a short report. Use a word processor program to prepare the heading and introduction for this report. The introduction should state the function of the spreadsheet and briefly how the results are worked out.

18 Use cut and paste (or a similar technique, depending on the software you are using), to transfer the spreadsheet results to the report. You may need to make adjustments to the layout in order to fit the results appropriately on the page. Add your own short commentary, describing briefly what the results show.

19 Save the report, preview and then obtain a printout.

20 Exit the word processor program.

Activity 5.7 Straight line depreciation

SITUATION

Set up a spreadsheet model to make depreciation calculations.

CONTENTS

Create spreadsheet model with more complex formulae; use absolute addressing in formalae; save to disk and adjust layout to fit on paper; include spreadsheet results in a report.

Level: ADVANCED

Elements: PREPARE, PROCESS INFORMATION

TASKS

1 Run the spreadsheet program on your system.

2 You are to create a spreadsheet model which will calculate the value of items of capital equipment (such as machines) and buildings after a number of years' depreciation. (Depreciation occurs when items lose value as they get older.)

You are to use straight line depreciation. This means that the value of the items decreases by the same amount each year.

Create a spreadsheet file with the layout shown in Fig. 7, and enter the data as shown.

Centre all the cells which are to be used below the heading.

3 Place a formula in B6 to calculate the annual depreciation. Base the formula on:

   original value / life of item.

4 Place a formula in cell B10 to make this cell contain the same as cell B4.

5 Place a formula in cell B11 to calculate the value at age 1 year.

6 You now need to use an absolute cell reference in order to copy the formula to the other rows in the spreadsheet. Edit the formula in B11 and change it to make the formula (when copied) always refer back to row 6 to pick up the annual depreciation in cell B6.

	A	B	C	D
1	**STRAIGHT LINE DEPRECIATION**			
2				
3	Item	Machine 1	Machine 2	Main building
4	Original value (£):	25 000	35 000	9 000 000
5	Life of item (yrs):	10	12	40
6	Annual depn. (£):			
7				
8	Value at age (yrs)			
9				
10	0			
11	1			
12	2			
13	3			
14	4			
15	5			
16	6			
17	7			
18	8			
19	9			
20	10			

Fig. 7

7 Copy this formula down to calculate the value at all the other ages.

8 Save the spreadsheet file to your own disk or your own user area under the file name DEPN1.

9 Copy the formulae in the range B10 : B20 to the same rows in columns C and D. You should now find that all the values for all three items have been calculated.

10 Display all the numbers in the spreadsheet to the nearest whole number.

11 Preview the printout of the spreadsheet, make any adjustments necessary to fit the printout on the paper, and print the spreadsheet.

12 Change the life of machine 2 to 8 years. Change the original value of the main building to £8 million. Print again.

13 Save the new version under the same file name (overwriting the previous file). Also make a back-up copy of the file under a different file name.

14 Print the final version of the spreadsheet. In your own handwriting, neatly label one column of figures, to show that the numbers have been set to display as whole numbers.

15 List on screen, and then print on paper, the files in the current directory, including the file names for this activity.

16 Exit the spreadsheet program.

17 You must now include your spreadsheet results in a short report. Use a word processor program to prepare the heading and introduction for this report. The introduction should state the function of the spreadsheet and briefly how the results are worked out.

18 Use cut and paste (or a similar technique, depending on the software you are using), to transfer the spreadsheet results to the report. You may need to make adjustments to the layout in order to fit the results appropriately on the page. Add your own short commentary, describing briefly what the results show.

19 Save the report, preview and then obtain a printout.

20 Exit the word processor program.

Activity 5.8 Reducing balance depreciation

SITUATION

Set up a spreadsheet model to make depreciation calculations

CONTENTS

Create spreadsheet model with more complex formulae; use absolute addressing in formalae. Save to disk and adjust layout to fit on paper; include spreadsheet results in a report.

Level: ADVANCED

Elements: PREPARE, PROCESS, PRESENT INFORMATION

	A	B	C	D
1	**REDUCING BALANCE DEPRECIATION**			
2				
3	Item	Machine 1	Machine 2	Main building
4	Original value (£):	25 000	35 000	9 000 000
5				
6	Depn. rate (%):	20	25	10
7				
8	Value at age (yrs)			
9				
10	0			
11	1			
12	2			
13	3			
14	4			
15	5			
16	6			
17	7			
18	8			
19	9			
20	10			

Fig. 8

TASKS

1 Run the spreadsheet program on your system.

2 You are to create a spreadsheet model which will calculate the value of items of capital equipment (such as machines) and buildings after a number of years' depreciation. (Depreciation occurs when items lose value as they get older.)

You are to use reducing balance depreciation. This means that the value of the item decreases each year by the same percentage of the value at the start of the year.

Create a spreadsheet file with the layout in Fig. 8, and enter the data as shown.

Centre all the cells which are to be used below the heading.

3 Place a formula in cell B10 to make this cell contain the same as cell B4.

4 Place a formula in cell B11 to calculate the value at age 1 year. This can be based on the following:

value this year = (value last year) × (100–depn. rate)/100.

5 You now need to use an absolute cell reference in order to copy the formula to the other rows in the spreadsheet. Edit the formula in B11 and change it to make the formula (when copied) always refer back to row 5 to pick up the depreciation rate per annum in cell B5.

6 Copy this formula down to calculate the value at all the other ages.

7 Save the spreadsheet file to your own disk or your own user area under the file name DEPN2.

8 Copy the formulae in the range B10 : B20 to the same rows in column C and D. You should now find that all the values for all three items have been calculated.

9 Display all the numbers in the spreadsheet to the nearest whole number.

10 Preview the printout of the spreadsheet, make any adjustments necessary to fit the printout on the paper, and print the spreadsheet.

11 Change the depreciation rate of machine 1 to 22%. Change the original value of machine 2 to £36 000. Print again.

12 Save the new version under the same file name (overwriting the previous file). Also make a back-up copy of the file under a different file name.

13 Print the final version of the spreadsheet. In your own handwriting, neatly label one column of figures, to show that the numbers have been set to display as whole numbers.

14 List on screen, and then print on paper, the files in the current directory, including the file names for this activity.

15 Exit the spreadsheet program.

16 You must now include your spreadsheet results in a short report. Use a word processor program to prepare the heading and introduction for this report. The introduction should state the function of the spreadsheet and briefly how the results are worked out.

17 Use cut and paste (or a similar technique, depending on the software you are using), to transfer the spreadsheet results to the report. You may need to make adjustments to the layout in order to fit the results appropriately on the page. Add your own short commentary, describing briefly what the results show.

18 Save the report, preview and then obtain a printout.

19 Exit the word processor program.

Activity 5.9

SITUATION

Set up a spreadsheet model to investigate the cash flow predictions of a business enterprise.

CONTENTS

Create spreadsheet model with more complex formulae; save to disk and adjust layout to fit on paper; include spreadsheet results in a report.

Level: ADVANCED

Elements: PREPARE, PROCESS, PRESENT INFORMATION

TASKS

1 Run the spreadsheet program.

2 You are to create a cash flow spreadsheet model to predict the end-of-month bank balance for a new business, given the amounts shown below of opening balance, income and expenditure:

The opening balance in January is £4000.

Income:
  Shop sales: Jan. – £500, Feb. – £600, Mar. – £800, Apr. – 1200, and £1500 per month from May onwards.
  Mail sales: Jan. – £100, Feb. £150, and £200 per month from March onwards.
  Other income: £50 per month.

Expenditure:
   Rent: £450 in Jan., Apr., Jul. and Oct.
   Council tax: £850 in Apr., Aug. and Dec.
   Wages: £600 each month.
   Equipment: Jan. – £2370, Feb. – £4100 and Aug. – £2100.
   Travel: £100 per month.
   Mailing: £25 per month.
   Electricity: £220 in Feb., May, Aug. and Nov.
   The cost of stock is estimated to be 25% of (shop sales + mail sales).
   Telephone: £57 per month.

Set up a suitable spreadsheet layout for these details (see p. 83 for an example). You will need a row to show opening balance each month, a row for every item of income and expenditure, and rows for the total income and total expenditure. The item headings should be placed down the first column and the months across the top row. Lock the spreadsheet cells containing text, to guard against accidental overtyping.

Once you have created the layout, fill the amounts in.

3 Place a formula to total the income for January. Copy the formula across to the other months.

4 Place a formula to total the expenditure for January. Copy the formula across to the other months.

5 Place a formula to calculate the monthly surplus for January. Copy the formula across to the other months.

6 Place a formula to calculate the closing balance for January. Copy the formula across to the other months. Place a formula in the opening balance row for February to carry forward the closing balance for January to become the opening balance for February. Copy this formula to the other months.

7 Save the spreadsheet model to your own disk or your own user area under the file name CFLOW1.

8 Print the cash flow spreadsheet. You should make the printout as compact as possible, preferably to fit on a sheet of A4 paper.

9 Freeze the titles so that the month name and the details in the first column remain on the screen while the rest of the spreadsheet scrolls.

10 The wage bill has gone up to £700 per month. Change this on the spreadsheet.

11 The bank manager insists that you will not be allowed to go into the red on your current account for any period of time; therefore you need a loan. Work out the amount of loan needed to bring you back into the black for the whole year, and put this loan in as income in January. The loan will be repaid in the following year.

12 Save the new version under the same file name (overwriting the previous file). Also make a back-up copy of the file under a different file name, and on a different drive or directory.

13 Print the final version of the spreadsheet. In your own handwriting, neatly label one column of figures, to show that the numbers have been right-aligned.

14 Select and then cut (or delete) the numbers in the spreadsheet which have not been calculated by formulae. Be careful not to delete the formulae. You should now be left with a blank template which can be kept for future use. Save this template under a suitable file name, and then print the blank spreadsheet.

15 List on screen, and then print on paper, the files in the current directory, including the file names for this activity.

16 Exit the spreadsheet program.

17 You must now include your spreadsheet results in a short report. Use a word processor program to prepare the heading and introduction for this report. The introduction should state the function of the spreadsheet and briefly how the results are worked out.

18 Use cut and paste (or a similar technique, depending on the software you are using), to transfer the spreadsheet results to the report. You may need to make adjustments to the layout in order to fit the results appropriately on the page. Add your own short commentary, describing briefly what the results show.

19 Save the report, preview and then obtain a printout.

20 Exit the word processor program.

6 Drawing

Background to drawing

Graphics software on a computer system may be used to create diagrams, pictures, charts and other images on the screen, and for printing onto paper. (For charts and graphs see Chapter 10.)

Drawing software

Some of the programs are available in different versions, according to the level of drawings which need to be produced, and the range of features which are needed. The range is wide, from the simple level of producing simple diagrams and pictures, to the professional level of using the computer for detailed design work.

Common drawing programs which are available for PCs include:

- Corel Draw
- Windows Paintbrush
- Autosketch
- AutoCad
- Professional Draw

Applications of drawing software

The business applications of drawing software can be split into two areas. The first area is the occasional use of the computer to produce a variety of diagrams and designs which do not require any specialist skill or qualifications in design work. The second area is the realm of the 'design professional'. Computer-aided design (CAD) software is available for this; the software offers a huge range of features, and many organisations who have a requirement for high accuracy design work employ professionals who work with the computer screen rather than on a drawing board as they would have done a few years ago. CAD software is often highly 'customised', that is, the organisation pays for the features which are required, to suit its requirements, rather than with most other forms of software where the package is a standard one.

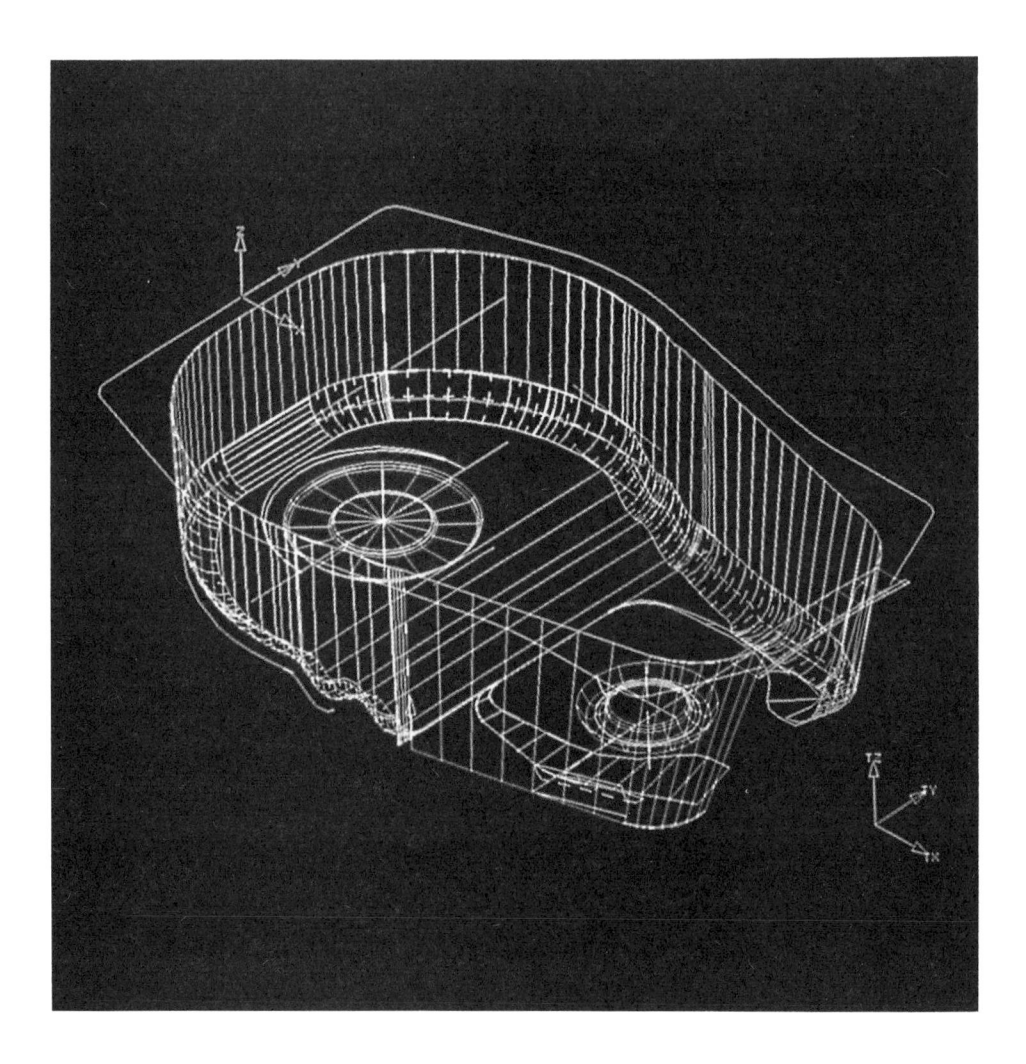

Fig. 9 Computer-aided design (CAD)

Most people can think of situations, either at home or in the course of their work, where a computer produced drawing would be useful. Examples of simple drawing programs are as follows.

■ Garden design

Garden design is possible with the aid of a personal computer equipped with drawing software and a good quality printer or plotter. The printer or plotter must be capable of producing graphics output. The shape of the garden may be shown on the computer screen, and then areas of flower beds, lawns, trees, patios and vegetable plot can be placed in suitable positions. The computer is used not just to print a neat copy of the design, but also to allow the user to experiment with alternative positions for the garden features.

Once the design has been completed, the printed or screen copy can be used to record progress as the structure and planting in the garden gets under way. A particular feature of the software used in this application is cut and paste (and copy), in which a garden object can be drawn, and then moved or copied to different parts of the garden.

■ Kitchen design

Special software exists which has been written for the task of kitchen design. Alternatively, a general purpose drawing program can be used quite successfully. The main task with kitchen design is to fit units such as cupboards, refrigerators and cookers into a limited space, while giving the best access to the person who will be using the kitchen. Again, cut and paste is useful here.

Most simple drawing programs will only really work in two dimensions. That is, you design the plan (from above) of the kitchen. It will usually be necessary to look also at the side views of the kitchen, and this is where a specific kitchen design program would be advantageous, since the kitchen is planned in three dimensions, so the user can see the appearance of the kitchen and its units from a variety of angles.

- **Office layout**

    Drawing programs enable an office to be properly planned, by moving objects to a variety of positions within the office until a satisfactory design is obtained.

- **Building floor plans**

    It is a common requirement in organisations to keep and update a plan of each floor of a particular building, to show the use of each room, its location, and the services, such as electrical sockets and computer cabling which is contained within it. A drawing program makes this a relatively easy job; once the initial plans have been stored it is a simple matter to make any alterations to them as they occur.

Hardware for drawing programs

Hardware requirements for graphics differ from those of other software which the user may experience. This is because graphics makes quite big demands on the processing power of the computer. For a PC in particular, the screen image will have to be sharp and accurate for professional design work, and there may be special requirements for the screen. For example, some drawing and design work needs a large screen which will display the information much more accurately than that required for other tasks such as word processing and spreadsheet work.

- **Processor**

    The processor for a drawing program should be powerful enough to carry out the large amount of processing which graphics software demands. A 286 or 386 processor will cope quite adequately with lower-end programs such as Windows Paintbrush, but for the more professional work, a 486 or Pentium processor is needed.

- **Disk storage**

    When you are using a drawing program, the data which represents the millions of pixels that make up the screen image have to be stored somewhere in the computer system. Some of this 'bit image' can be kept in the RAM of the computer, and changes which are made to the picture can be effected quickly to areas of the picture that are stored in the RAM. However, even the most modern PCs have some difficulty in dealing with the whole of the screen image in the RAM quickly enough to respond to changes which the user is making to the picture. Therefore, much of the picture will be stored in temporary files on hard disk (or network drives).

This has two important effects. First, the area of disk storage available to the drawing program for these temporary files must be large enough. The user should make sure, for example, that there is always spare capacity on the hard disk before any important drawing work is started. Secondly, the faster the disk operates, the better the system will be able to respond to commands. To use a drawing program which takes a long time to make changes on the screen can be extremely frustrating and time consuming, and this will be the result if the disk drive is not up to the job.

■ Monitor

The monitor for a drawing program has to give a sharp image, and it needs to be colour for most applications. A variety of graphics standards can be supported by the program, for example VGA and Super VGA at various resolutions.

■ Printer

A laser printer, or possibly a plotter, is needed for a realistic paper version of the image that you have designed on the screen. The design of the dot matrix printer does not suit the drawing on paper of lines and shaded areas, although printouts can be made to virtually all dot matrix printers. The quality from these will not be good.

■ Mouse

A mouse or other similar device is essential for drawing on computer. The device is used to point to positions on the screen and to move objects from one area of the picture to another, and this cannot be done effectively with only a keyboard. However, the user may find a mouse rather uncomfortable for long periods of time, as it can produce an ache in the hand, wrist or arm.

Other devices can be used as alternatives to a mouse, such as a light pen or a roller ball.

Features offered by drawing programs

The range of possible features in any drawing program is huge, depending upon the level of software which is being used. For this reason, we shall cover the most basic type of software, such as Windows Paintbrush. Any simple drawing program can offer the following range of features.

■ **Select line width**

If lines are to be drawn on a picture, the user should firstly fix the width of the lines. This is usually done by selecting from a scale of line widths in the toolbox area of the screen. The toolbox is used to choose which tool or operation is to be done next.

■ **Draw straight lines**

The mouse is clicked to fix the starting and ending position of a line. It may be possible to alter the length or angle of the line once drawn; it will certainly be possible to remove it.

■ **Draw curved lines**

In order to join up two points on the picture with a curved line, the start and end points are first fixed by clicking the mouse. This will generally produce a line on the picture which is straight to begin with. Then, however, you drag the mouse to introduce curves in the line to match the picture element required.

■ **Draw rectangles**

By clicking the mouse the two opposite corners of a rectangle can be fixed on to the picture. The corners of the rectangle may be square or curved, depending upon the tool which has been chosen. The shape may be in outline form or filled with colour.

- **Draw ellipse or circle**

    A circle is a special case of an ellipse or oval figure, which can be included in a picture. You fix the shape and size of the ellipse by clicking on the centre of the shape and then on one of the corners of the ellipse or circle. The shape may be in outline form or filled with colour.

- **Draw freehand lines**

    Instead of using the mouse to fix the starting and ending points of the lines in your picture, you can use the mouse like a paintbrush or pen to draw the lines freehand. Again, it is important to select the right width of paintbrush to begin with, and most programs will allow you to vary the shape of the brush or nib, to produce interesting effects. This feature is most easily used with a pen attachment instead of a mouse.

- **Paint fill**

    If the picture on the screen has an area which is entirely enclosed, you may fill the area with colour. Generally, select your colour first from the palette by clicking on the colour required, then position the point of the tool inside the area to be filled and click. You must be very careful here to ensure that the area is entirely enclosed; if not, the colour may spill out of the area to other parts of your picture where you did not want it. If this happens, use the **<Undo>** feature of the program, which undoes the last operation (and generally only the last operation).

- **Edit palette**

    The colours which are used can be changed, either by selecting from a range of palette files on disk, or by mixing together colours to produce new colours. It is possible to edit individual pixels (picture elements) to mix the colours.

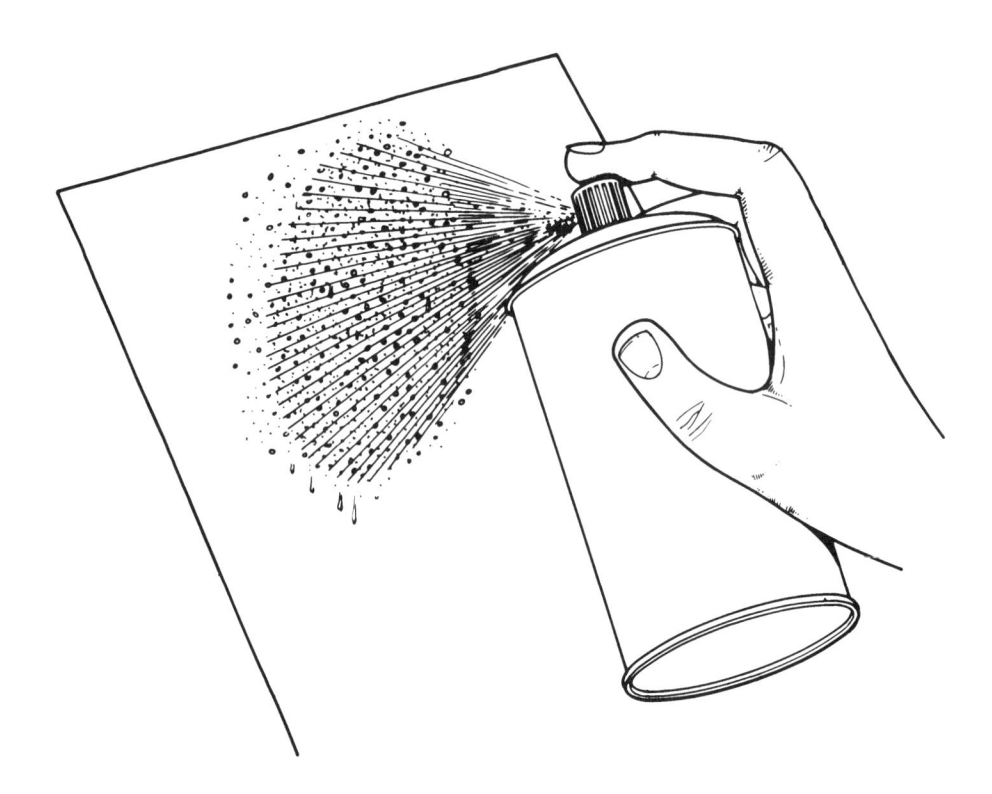

■ Spray can

A variety of interesting effects may be added to your picture, depending on the software in use. A spray can is usually available. This tool mimics the use of a real can of spray paint, and takes some skill to use properly. It is usually possible to edit the pattern of points of colour which are produced from the tool.

■ Text

Text may be written on the picture in a variety of font shapes and sizes. Once the text is on the picture you can add effects, such as reflecting, enlarging or tilting the text. The more advanced drawing programs will enable the user to make virtually any changes to the text that one can think of.

■ Flip, shrink, grow and tilt

By cutting out areas of the picture, you can carry out transformations of them, such as enlarging or reducing them in size. Or, for example, a rectangular area, once selected, can be copied to another part of the screen, but its shape and size can be changed by clicking on the corners of the new rectangle.

■ Eraser

An eraser is available to rub out details of the picture. As with the paintbrush itself, the size of the tool can be changed.

Activity 6.1

SITUATION

Draw a set of simple shapes.

CONTENTS

Draw simple shapes; select tools and vary the effects of tools; save to disk, print to fit paper.

Level: INTERMEDIATE

Elements: PROCESS, PRESENT INFORMATION

TASKS

1 Run the drawing program on your system.

2 Use the appropriate tools, with a suitable line thickness to draw the following shapes:

- rectangle;
- square;
- triangle;
- lines.

3 Select the cut-out tool, draw a cut-out around the rectangle and move it to another area of the drawing surface.

4 Select the cut-out tool, draw a cut-out around the triangle, and copy it to two other areas of the drawing surface.

5 Select the cut-out tool, draw a cut-out around the square, and delete it.

6 Select the eraser tool, choose a suitable thickness for the eraser, and erase the vertical straight line.

7 Save the picture to your own disk or your own user area under the file name SHAPES1.

8 Preview the printout of the drawing, make any adjustments necessary in order to obtain a satisfactory printout, and print the drawing.

9 Exit the drawing program.

Activity 6.2

SITUATION

Draw a set of simple shapes.

CONTENTS

Draw simple shapes; select tools and vary the effects of tools; save to disk, print to fit paper.

Level: INTERMEDIATE

Elements: PROCESS, PRESENT INFORMATION

TASKS

1 Run the drawing program on your system.

2 Use the appropriate tools, with a suitable line thickness to draw the following shapes.

- small circle;
- large circle;

- filled rectangle;
- freehand shape.

3 Select the cut-out tool, draw a cut-out around the filled rectangle, select the enlarge feature and draw an enlarged version of the original filled rectangle.

4 Select the cut-out tool, draw a cut-out around the large circle, select the reduce feature, and draw a reduced version of the original circle.

5 Select the spray can tool, and lightly spray the freehand shape.

6 Select the zoom-in tool, choose an area of the freehand shape, and edit some of the pixels in this area individually.

7 Save the picture to your own disk or your own user area under the file name SHAPES2.

8 Preview the printout of the drawing, make any adjustments necessary in order to obtain a satisfactory printout, and print the drawing.

9 Exit the drawing program.

Activity 6.3

SITUATION

Draw and manipulate a set of shapes.

CONTENTS

Draw shapes; select tools and vary the effects of tools; save to disk; print to fit paper; use cut-and-paste to achieve movement, copying and transformation.

Level: INTERMEDIATE

Elements: PROCESS, PRESENT INFORMATION

TASKS

1 Run the drawing program on your system.

2 Select the rectangle drawing tool. Set the line width to thin lines. Set the rectangle tool so that the rectangles drawn are in outline, not filled with colour.

3 Draw a rectangle in the top half of the screen.

4 Select the circle drawing tool. Set the circle tool so that circles will be filled with red colour.

5 Draw a circle in the centre of the rectangle.

6 Select the rectangular cut-out tool and cut around the rectangle.

7 Use the cut-and-paste or copy-and-paste feature to make another copy of the rectangle and circle in the bottom half of the screen.

8 Save the file to your own disk or your own user area under the file name REDCIRC.

9 Select the rectangular cut-out tool and cut around the top rectangle.

10 Select the 'shrink and grow' tool, and make the rectangle smaller in size.

11 Select the rectangular cut-out tool and cut around the bottom rectangle.

12 Select the 'tilt' tool and make the rectangle change shape.

13 Select the text tool and set the font to a large size.

14 Put the title 'Changing shape' near the top of the drawing.

15 Save the file under the same file name, overwriting the previous version.

16 Preview the printout of the picture, make any adjustments necessary and obtain a printout.

17 Exit the drawing program.

Activity 6.4

SITUATION

Draw and manipulate a set of shapes.

CONTENTS

Draw shapes; select tools and vary the effects of tools; save to disk, print to fit paper; use cut-and-paste to achieve movement, copying and transformation.

Level: INTERMEDIATE

Elements: PROCESS, PRESENT INFORMATION

TASKS

1 Run the drawing program on your system.

2 Select the rectangle drawing tool. Set the line width to thin lines. Set the rectangle tool so that the rectangles drawn are in outline, not filled with colour.

3 Draw a square in the top half of the screen.

4 Select the straight line tool. Draw a straight line across each diagonal. Zoom in on one corner of the square to check that the diagonal line meets the corner of the square exactly. If it does not, use the pixel editing feature to make it meet. Zoom out to see the drawing in its previous size.

5 Repeat the examination of each corner of the square.

6 Select the paint fill tool. Choose a blue colour for the paint fill. Fill one quarter of the square with blue colour.

7 In the same way, fill the other three quarters of the square with red, green and yellow.

8 Select the rectangular cut-out tool and cut around the square.

9 Use the cut-and-paste or copy-and-paste feature to make another copy of the square in the bottom half of the screen.

10 Select the rectangular cut-out tool and cut around one of the squares. Now use the flip feature to flip the square over vertically, and note the change in the positions of the coloured quadrants of the square.

11 Save the file to your own disk or your own user area under the file name SQUARE.

12 Put the title 'Coloured square' near the top of the drawing

13 Save the file under the same file name, overwriting the previous version.

14 Preview the printout of the picture, make any adjustments necessary and obtain a printout.

15 Exit the drawing program.

Activity 6.5 Garden design 1

SITUATION

Produce a garden design for Greenscape Garden Designs.

CONTENTS

Produce a complex drawing with a variety of effects; save to disk and print to fit paper.

Level: ADVANCED

Elements: PROCESS, PRESENT INFORMATION

TASKS

1 Run the drawing program on your system.

2 Set the drawing surface to A4 portrait size.

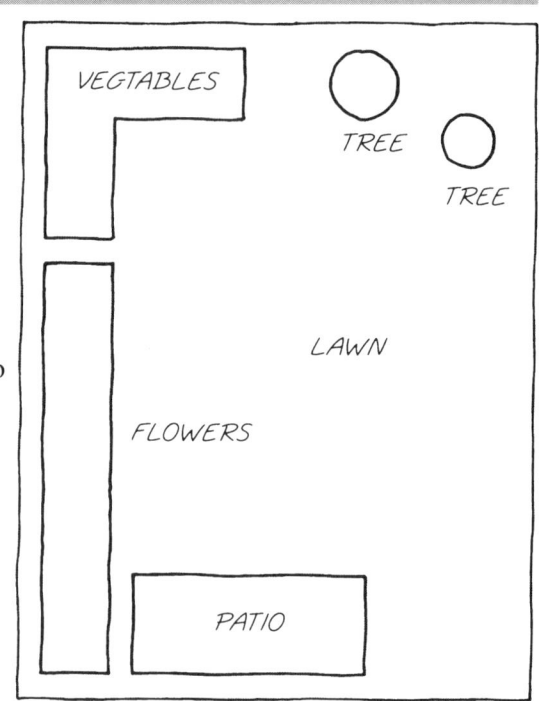

3 Draw a large rectangle, covering most of the drawing surface, but leaving a gap above for a title, to represent the garden area.

4 Place the title: 'Greenscape Garden Designs' at the top of the drawing surface.

5 Draw a single rectangular vegetable plot at the top (far end) of the garden. Label this with the text 'Vegetables'.

6 At the bottom (near end) of the garden, place a rectangular patio area. Label this with the text 'Patio'.

7 On the left-hand side of the garden, leaving a gap both ends before the patio and the vegetable plot, place a rectangular flower border. Label this with the text 'Flowers'.

8 Position two trees, represented by outline circles, at suitable positions on the right of the garden and towards the far end. Label each of these with the text 'Tree'.

9 The rest of the garden is to be turfed. Label this with the text 'Lawn'.

10 Save the drawing to your own disk or your own user area under the file name GARDEN1.

11 Preview the printout of the drawing, make any adjustments necessary and obtain a printout.

12 Exit the drawing program.

Activity 6.6 Garden design 2

SITUATION

Amend a garden design for Greenscape Garden Designs.

CONTENTS

Retrieve a drawing from disk; add a variety of effects; save to disk and print to fit paper.

Level: ADVANCED

Elements: PROCESS, PRESENT INFORMATION

TASKS

1 Run the drawing program on your system.

2 Retrieve the file GARDEN1 from your own disk or your own user area.

3 Check that the shapes representing objects within the garden are fully enclosed, so that the colour-fill tool can be used. If necessary, use the zoom-in tool to fill any gaps to make the shapes fully enclosed.

4 Fill the vegetable plot with a brown colour.

5 Fill the trees with a dark green colour.

6 Fill the patio with a red colour.

7 Fill the lawn with a light green colour.

8 Fill the flower border with a yellow colour.

9 Select the curved line tool. Set the line width for this tool to a very thick line, suitable for drawing a curved path down the length of the garden.

10 Select a grey colour for this tool.

11 Draw a path, using the curved line tool, down the garden from the patio to the vegetable plot, towards the left-hand side of the garden.

12 Make any adjustments necessary to your drawing by using the zoom-in and pixel editing tools.

13 Preview the printout of the drawing, make any adjustments necessary to obtain a satisfactory printout and print it.

14 If a colour printer is available, select this and print to it, otherwise print to your usual printer.

15 Save the file to your own disk or you own user area under the new file name GARDEN2.

16 Exit the drawing program.

Activity 6.7 Layout of reception area

SITUATION

Produce a design for the layout of Sportstown Leisure Centre's reception area.

CONTENTS

Produce a complex drawing, approximately to scale and with a variety of effects; save to disk and print to fit paper.

Level: ADVANCED

Elements: PROCESS, PRESENT INFORMATION

TASKS

1 Run the drawing program on your system.

2 Create a new drawing and set the line width to a small size. If the

drawing program has a ruler feature, switch this on so that objects can be drawn approximately to scale. If the program does not have a ruler, do the best you can to make the scale of the objects match the actual sizes given.

3 Draw a rectangle to represent the reception area of Sportstown Leisure Centre. It measures 10 × 14 metres. Show the 14-metre side of the rectangle horizontally across the screen.

4 Draw one of the units which make up the reception counter as a rectangle which measures 1 × 2 metres. By using the cut-and-paste or copying feature of your drawing program, place three of these counter units next to each other to make a counter which measures 1 × 6 metres.

5 Cut out the complete counter and place it along a 14-metre wall of the reception area, but with a gap to the same wall of 2 metres.

6 Draw a circle of diameter 2.5 metres to represent a display stand, which is also to be positioned in the reception area, near to the other 14-metre wall. Copy this display stand and place another one next to it.

7 Save the file to your own disk or your own user area under the file name RECEPT1.

8 Preview the printout of the drawing, make any adjustments necessary, and print it.

9 A special hard-wearing section of carpet is to be laid in the reception area, immediately in front of the counter. Draw this as a rectangle measuring 6 × 2 metres.

10 Place text labels of suitable size against the reception counter, the display stands and the carpet, and title the complete drawing 'Sportstown Leisure Centre Reception Area'.

11 Save the new version of the drawing, overwriting the previous version.

12 Preview the printout, make any adjustments necessary and print it.

13 Exit the drawing program.

Activity 6.8 Office design for Wessex Windows

SITUATION

Produce a design for the information systems room at Wessex Windows.

CONTENTS

Produce a complex drawing, approximately to scale and with a variety of effects; save to disk and print to fit paper.

Level: ADVANCED

Elements: PROCESS, PRESENT INFORMATION

TASKS

1 Run the drawing program on your system.

2 Create a new drawing and set the line width to a small size. If the drawing program has a ruler feature, switch this on so that objects can be drawn approximately to scale. If the program does not have a ruler, do the best you can to make the scale of the objects match the actual sizes given.

3 Draw a rectangle to represent the information systems rooms at Wessex Windows regional office. It measures 12 × 15 metres. Show the 15-metre side of the rectangle horizontally across the screen.

4 Draw a rectangle to represent a single desk, which measures 1.75 × 0.9 metres. By using the cut-and-paste or copying feature of your drawing program, place six of these desks next to each other along one side of the room, allowing a gap of 1 metre between the desks and the wall. Using cut-and-paste, copy this row of six desks to the other long side of the room.

5 Mark on the left-hand wall (as you look at it on the screen) the door opening. This is in the middle of the length of the 12 metre wall. The opening is 0.9 metre wide, and should be shown on your drawing by two short, horizontal lines crossing the line of the wall.

Drawing

6 Draw a small, filled square to represent a computer, equivalent to a size of 0.6 metres square. Use cut-and-paste to copy the computer to six of the desks, three on each side of the room.

7 Save the file to your own disk or your own user area under the file name INFROOM1.

8 Preview the printout of the drawing, make any adjustments necessary, and print it.

9 Alter your drawing to try another room layout, with the 12 desks arranged in four groups of three, placed in appropriate positions in the room. Each 'island' of three desks should make an L-shape.

10 Place text labels of suitable size door opening and desk islands, and title the complete drawing: 'Wessex Windows Information Centre'.

11 Save the new version of the drawing, overwriting the previous version.

12 Preview the printout, make any adjustments necessary and print it.

13 Exit the drawing program.

7 Microsoft Windows

Definition

Microsoft Windows is a set of programs which provide a graphical user interface for MS–DOS on personal computers.

Versions

There have been a number of versions of Microsoft Windows. Earlier versions were not so widely used, but when Microsoft released Windows 3.0, it was extremely successful, and became a standard on many PCs across the world.

Windows 3.1 included considerable improvements on the previous version, and the trend continues with further versions including Windows for Workgroups and Windows 95. Windows for Workgroups is designed to allow groups of users to work together on computer networks. The aim is that files can be shared, and networks used in an efficient way for access to common information and for communicating. Windows 95 (released in 1995) is a further improvement, and incorporates the operating system as well as communications software.

Background to 'Windows'

To the user, the chief advantage of operating on a computer with Windows installed is that the computer is easier to use. The graphical user interface that it provides allows the user to move a mouse to point to menus and choose commands rather than to have to remember the correct format of the command to type in. All the options should be available on the screen at any time. It is thought by many people that Windows presents a more natural way of working with a computer.

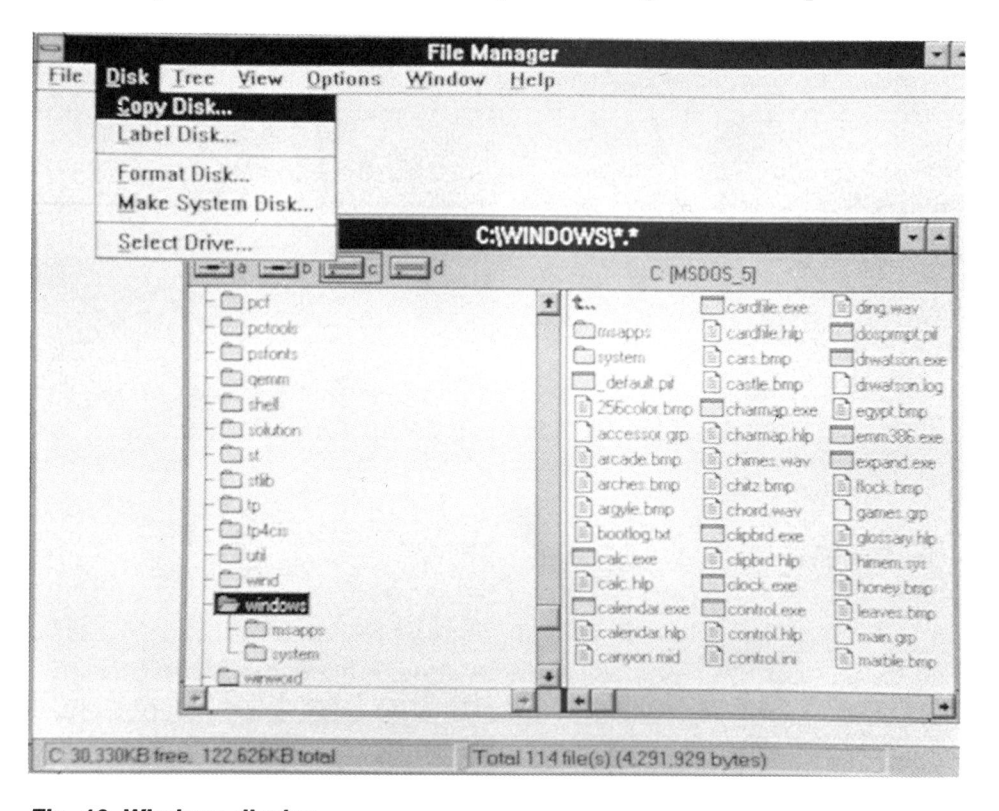

Fig. 10 Windows display

'Program Manager'

The first Windows element which runs when Windows is started is called the 'Program Manager'. This is the only program which runs continuously, all the time that Windows is running in the computer. A lot of the time it will be running in the background, while the user is, for example, operating a spreadsheet program.

Program Manager is used for launching the applications or other programs which are on the computer system. Usually, the programs are shown individually on the screen as icons – small pictures or symbols to represent the program. For example a database program can be represented as a filing cabinet icon, since the function of a database program is to store and give access to information in the same way that a filing cabinet does. Each icon can be labelled with the name of the program underneath. In addition to program icons, it is possible to show other files as icons. For example, a spreadsheet which has been developed to calculate and record staff travelling expenses can be saved as a disk file, and shown in Program Manager as a separate icon.

The individual icons, representing the programs available on the computer system are placed into groups. A group contains files and programs of similar type. For example, you could have a group called 'Applications', containing all the main applications programs which are available on the system. A second group may be called 'Housekeeping', and this could contain programs, utilities and files which are used to maintain the system; for example, facilities for making backup copies of files and programs to check for viruses on the system. A third group might be games.

All these alternatives are the choices of the person who configures or sets up the system. With a stand-alone PC this may be the user himself; on a local area network the system or network manager would be the one to make these decisions. Any new programs or files which are going to be used have to be set up within Program Manager. This is a fairly easy task; it is simply a matter of telling Program Manager to set up a new icon, what it is called, what group it is to be included in, and what directory the main files and data files it uses are to be found in. Most new applications programs will include an icon to use within Windows. If this is not the case, simple programs are available for the user to design his or her own icons.

'Windows'

The program gets its name from the windows on the screen which can contain different tasks. Every time a task is run it operates within a window. This window might fill the whole screen, just half of it, or even a relatively small area of the screen. It is possible to operate two applications programs at the same time.

For example, you may want to do some calculations on staff travelling expenses in a spreadsheet program, and then to write a memo to staff on the word processor to query some of the expense claims they have made. To do this you could run the spreadsheet, close it down when you have finished the calculations, make a note of the relevant figures, then open a word processor file and type up the memo. With Windows, however, this might not be the most efficient way of doing things. You can have spreadsheet and word processor programs running in two halves of the screen at the same time, and switch between the two when needed by clicking the mouse.

■ Task switching

Even if you do not need to have both windows on the screen at the same time, it can be useful to have both programs running at the same time. You can then very quickly switch from one program to the other without having to wait for the relatively slow process of closing down one program and starting up the other. Task switching, as Windows calls it, is an efficient way of working.

■ Changing the size of a window

When you run a program in a window, you can decide on the size of the window, and on the position of the window on the screen. In the right-hand corner of the window, buttons are available to alter its size. A maximise button (upward pointing arrow), when clicked, will make the window as large as possible. A minimise button (downward pointing arrow), when clicked, will reduce the task to an icon. If this is done, you may double-click on the icon to bring the window back to its previous size. Sometimes a button with both up and down arrows on it will be shown; if this is clicked, the window returns to its previous size.

Finally, to change the size of a window you can also move the mouse pointer to a corner of the window and drag the corner in or out. This will have the effect of changing its size or shape.

■ Moving a window

If a window does not occupy the whole of the area available to it, you can move the whole window to another position on the screen. This is done by placing the mouse pointer over the banner at the top of the window (where the name of the task appears) and dragging it across the screen.

- **Multiple windows**

    If you have more than one window on the screen at the same time, you can decide how the windows appear. To show one window in front of another so that they overlap, use 'Window Cascade' from the menus. Newly opened windows will appear in front of existing ones. To divide up the screen area available, giving the same amount of space to each window, use the 'Window Tile' options from the menus.

'File Manager'

'File Manager' is the Windows program which enables you to keep files in an organised way. The File Manager is run from Program Manager by clicking on its icon. When it runs, you will be able to view lists of files, directory tree structures and other details for any disk drives available on your system. File Manager can be configured as you wish. For example, you may want to view the files on the hard disk drive C in the top half of the screen, and the file on floppy disk, drive A in the bottom half. This is done by opening two windows and using the 'Window Tile' options from the menus.

There is a choice of information to view when looking at files. On some occasions you may want to see just the file name and date of last modification to the file for all the files in a sub-directory. At another time it may be that you need to see the size of the file (in bytes) and the file attributes. These choices are available from the menus in File Manager.

In addition, you can have the files in a list sorted into different orders, according to the file name, the type of file, the size of file or the date the file was last modified. An example of the use of this is when you are looking for all the files you previously created with your word processor program; you can sort them into file type order. All the files created in the word processor will now be grouped together, according to the three-letter file name extension. (For example, Word Perfect documents may be grouped together because they all have the file name extension 'WPS'.)

Other 'Windows' accessories

A number of other accessories are provided with the Windows programs as follows.

Notepad

This is a small word processor or text editor program. It is mainly used for editing text files, such as the batch files and configuration files which fix certain aspects of how a system is set up; for example the **autoexec.bat** and **config.sys** files. These should not be edited by users unless they know exactly what they are doing, or else the system setting can be so altered as to make programs unusable.

Also, the Notepad program may be used as a word processor in its own right, but it has limited facilities.

Windows Write

This is a genuine word processor program which has a WYSIWYG ('What you see is what you get') display. It shows the actual shape and size of characters on the screen when the font is changed, but it misses out a lot of the features of a more powerful word processor.

Paintbrush

This is a simple drawing program, and is suitable for carrying out the task described in the chapter on Drawing software.

Calendar

A calendar program is provided to keep track of the dates and times of appointments.

Calculator

This is useful for quick calculations on the screen, and it simulates the appearance of an actual hand-held calculator. It may be set to scientific or normal mode.

Clock

Many users keep the clock permanently displayed on the screen (in a corner where it will not get in the way of anything else), and it can be set to display times in analogue or digital forms.

Activity 7.1 Using Windows File Manager

SITUATION

Use Windows 3.1 File Manager to view and manipulate files.

CONTENTS

View files and directories; display directory structures; move, copy and delete files, both individually and in groups.

Levels: INTERMEDIATE, ADVANCED

Element: PROCESS INFORMATION

TASKS

1 Run Microsoft Windows.

2 Run File Manager by double-clicking the mouse button on the File Manager icon.

3 If File Manager does not fill the whole of the current window, make it do so by clicking the mouse pointer on the maximise button (up arrow) in the top right-hand corner of the window.

4 From the menu bar, choose **<View>, <Tree and Directory>**. This will display the directory tree in the left of the window, and the file list in the right of the window.

5 Click the mouse pointer on the root directory icon in the directory tree. Note that all the sub-directories and files in the root directory appear in the right of the window.

6 Sort the file list into different orders. This is done by selecting **<View>**

from the menu bar, and then either **<Sort by Name>**, **<Sort by Type>**, **<Sort by Size>** or **<Sort by Date>**.

7 From the menu bar choose **<Tree>**, **<Expand all>**. This will show the full directory structure on the currently selected drive. Click the mouse pointer on the root directory of the tree, and from the menu bar choose **<Tree>**, **<Collapse branch>**. This will have the opposite effect.

8 Double-click the mouse pointer on the root directory icon to expand the tree to the next level. Double-click the mouse pointer on a sub-directory icon to expand that sub-directory to the next level. Notice that the file list changes to show the files in the currently selected sub-directory.

9 Double-click the mouse pointer again on the same sub-directory icon to collapse that branch.

10 Choose a sub-directory containing some word-processed or other documents that can be moved or copied without damaging the integrity of your system. Do *not* choose a directory which contains program files. If in doubt, ask for advice from your lecturer. Expand the branch. Sort the file list by name. Pick out one file and move it to another sub-directory by dragging the file name icon with the mouse pointer across to the destination sub-directory in the left of the window. List the files in the destination sub-directory to check that the file has been moved. Now move the file back to its original location.

11 Now copy a document file from one location to another. This is done by dragging the file name in the same way, but with the **<CTRL>** (control) key held down at the same time.

12 From the menu bar choose **<Window>**, **<New window>**, and then **<Window>**, **<Tile>**. These two operations will open an extra window within File Manager and place the two windows next to one another to file the File Manager window area.

13 Do not make any changes in the upper window. In the lower window, click the mouse pointer on a different disk drive icon. (If you click on drive A you must have a floppy disk in drive A.) This will give you one disk drive as the current drive in the upper window and a different drive as the current drive in the lower window, and the procedure may be used for copying files from one drive to another. Backups of files can be created or updated in this way.

14 Drag a file from the right half of the upper window and place it on a sub-directory in the left half of the lower window. The file will be copied into its new location, leaving the original in place.

15 Select a number of files in the right of the upper window to copy to a sub-directory in the left of the lower window. This is done by holding down the **<SHIFT>** key as you click on the file names in order to select adjacent files. To select non-adjacent files, use the **<CTRL>** key while you click on the file name. When you have finished your selection, drag all the files across in one movement. Check that the files have been copied.

16 Delete the copies of the files on the destination disk drive by selecting them and pressing the **<Delete>** key. You will be asked to confirm deletion of the files. (Deleting files should be done with care.)

17 Close File Manager by double-clicking the mouse pointer on the File Manager top left-hand button.

18 Exit Windows by double-clicking the mouse pointer on the Program Manager top left-hand button.

8 Database

Background to database

A database is a computerised means of storing information in a structured way, so that information may be recalled, rearranged and output in the most flexible way possible. The key to the use of a database program

Fig. 11 Manual filing

is in making the data easy and quick to get at, and simple to manipulate. The database system is made up of three elements: the software, the hardware (computer, printer, etc.) and the user.

Software for database

▶▶ FIND OUT

> Find out what database software you are to use on your system. Find out also how to run the database program on your system. You also need access to a user manual, any tutorial package that is available, and, preferably the help of a lecturer/tutor if you have difficulties.

Some of the best-known database programs for personal computers are shown below:

- Access
- Paradox
- Dataease
- dBASE IV
- Foxpro
- Clipper

As with other software, there are DOS-based and Windows-based versions available. In addition, the programs are updated fairly frequently by the software manufacturers, so that each successive version will operate in a slightly different way. You need to check on the precise version of the software you are using before you get help from a manual or lecturer/tutor.

Situation

Some of the information and activities in this chapter will relate to the work of John Snowdon, a sales consultant for Wessex Windows. Wessex Windows manufacture, sell and fit single and double-glazed window and door units to both residential and commercial properties in the south of England.

John Snowdon's job entails establishing and then following up contacts in the area who may be interested in a quotation for replacement doors and windows. Once the quotation has been prepared and given, John then attempts to make the sale. If a sale is agreed, he arranges a time for the surveyor to visit the property to take precise measurements. These measurements are then entered into a computer system at the factory and a detailed job specification is output from the computer. This tells the factory engineers how to produce the windows and doors for a particular customer.

When the units have been fitted, John has then to make arrangements for payment for the work. This is either one cash sum or a series of instalments. There is of course an accounts department at head office, but John Snowdon makes the preliminary arrangements and also follows up any further problems with late payments.

John Snowdon makes full use of computers. He carries with him a laptop PC, and this provides the means of calculating the quotation for the

Fig. 12 Laptop PC

customer. An internally fitted modem means that he can use a telephone socket to transfer information to or from head office while 'on the road'.

Several software packages are installed on the PC, one of which is a database program that has been set up to store a large amount of information on past, current and future customers. An important feature of Wessex Windows is that there is a strong belief amongst the staff that the product is actually the best on the market, and therefore it is worthwhile keeping in contact with customers who have already had work done to see if they require further work carrying out in the future.

Basic features of database

A database program can be considered to be an electronic version of a filing cabinet, but this underestimates the power of the database. You can do more with a database than just store and recall records. The real power of the database is in the extremely flexible way the computer will let you manipulate information.

To learn how to use a database program you first need to understand how the data is to be stored inside the computer and on disk. Each file that you create will have a particular file structure.

For example, John Snowdon keeps a list of all his past, present and potential customers in a database file. The file is stored on the hard disk drive of his laptop PC, and two backup copies of the file are kept in a safe place. In the customer file there is one record for each customer. This is equivalent to having one card for each customer in a manual card index system. Each record consists of a number of different items. These items are called fields. Although these fields contain different information for each customer, each record has the same fields. The fields in John Snowdon's customer database file are:

- Customer number
- Surname
- First name or initials
- Address
- Home telephone number
- Work telephone number

- Date of first contact
- Date of most recent contact
- Job number of work done (or to be done)
- Job number of subsequent work done (or to be done)
- Further visit required
- Notes

All of these items of information are fields. All the fields relating to one customer are grouped together in a record. All the customers' records together are stored in a file.

Two significant advantages to John of keeping these customer records in

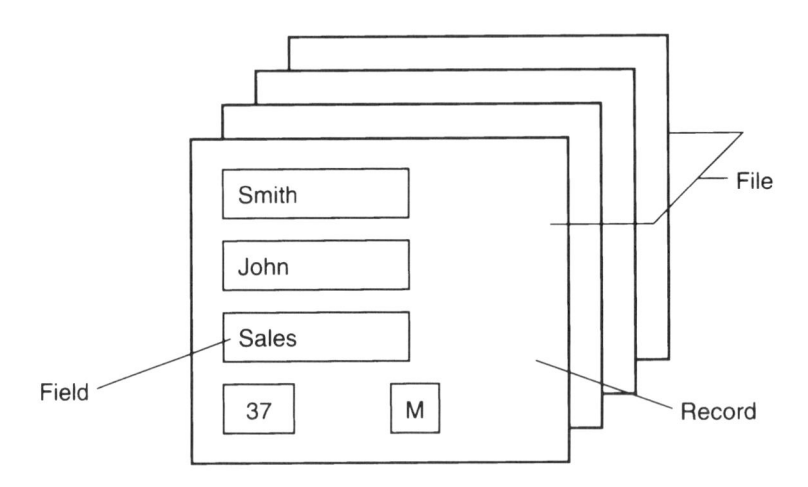

Fig. 13 Database file structure

a computer database file are the speed of retrieval and the saving of space. Effectively, John carries his filing cabinet around with him when he is on the road, and, once the machine has been turned on and the database application run, it takes a few seconds at most to find the details of one customer.

For very large files, a user of a database file may notice a slow-down in the speed of retrieval, because of the large amount of processing which may be required inside the computer in order to find or update a record. This will depend to a great extent on the performance of the computer. A PC with a fast processor, such as a 486 or Pentium will operate on large files noticeably more quickly than one with an older, slower processor such as an 8086, 286 or 386.

Another factor is the speed at which the hard disk drive operates. When the computer is attempting to find or update a record from amongst a large number of other records, the time taken for the disk drive read/write heads to move across the surface of the disk, and the time taken to physically read or write the data itself, will be major factors in the speed of operation (and thus usefulness) of the database program.

Operation of database

■ Create file structure

The first task to be done on the computer when starting a new file with a database program is to create the structure of the database. Most (but not all) database programs require the user to specify exactly what information is to be stored. The user will specify the field names (for example, the list of fields above), and usually the field types and widths. The field type describes the type of information to be stored under that field name. A typical choice of field types for a particular database program is as follows:

- Numeric (e.g. the customer reference number).
- Text (e.g. the customer's surname).
- Date (e.g. the date of first contact with the customer).
- Memo (e.g. for longer passages of text, the notes filed in the customer database file).
- Logical (i.e. a field containing values which are either 'true' or 'false', such as the 'Further visit required' field in the customer database. This would essentially contain either 'Yes' or 'No').

■ Screen forms

Once the file structure has been created, the user is then able to set up a screen display. The display will need to be clearly set out on the screen, so that the entry of data and recalling of information is easy for anyone who uses the file. With most database programs, any number of screen displays can be created; you may, for example, have one display for entering new data, another for editing existing data, and another for viewing lists of customers.

■ Add records

A large proportion of time with most database files will be spent in adding new data to the file. This may be done by adding extra records to the end of the file or by inserting the records into particular positions between other records.

■ Delete records

From time to time some records will need to be deleted. Deletion of records must be done with care, and all database programs have safeguards, so that the user is offered the chance to back out of a command to delete a record in case it was done in error. However, an extra safeguard should always be taken by the user, by keeping a backup copy of the file which can be used if something goes wrong in any particular session.

■ Edit records

Editing of records needs to be done speedily. In a large file, it becomes important to be able to call up the records to be edited quickly, either by scrolling through a list on the screen in a certain order, or by searching for records which match some condition. John Snowdon edits customer records by keying in their customer reference number. This field is indexed in his database file, so that the computer is able to find a record by its customer reference number very quickly.

■ Sort records

In a filing cabinet, records are kept in one particular order, and this order does not change. In fact, it is a vital part of the upkeep of a paper filing system to ensure that records are always replaced in the filing cabinet in their correct position. If this is not done it becomes difficult to find records.

However, in a computer database file, the records, though they may by physically stored on the surface of the hard disk in one order, can be rearranged on the screen or on paper in any order required. For example, John Snowdon frequently sorts his customer database file into customer reference number order when he is arranging for the surveyor to visit customers who have placed an order for work to be done. On other occasions he wants to view the file in order of the date of the most recent contact; this is so that he can contact past customers on a regular basis to check whether they require any more work to be done.

■ Retrieve individual records

Calling up records individually is one of the most useful aspect of a database file, and it is done by entering a search condition. John Snowdon keys in the customer number he requires; the computer then searches through the records in the file until it finds the customer with the required number; the record is then displayed on the screen.

■ Select a list of records

With a manual, paper filing system the records must be viewed one at a time. In a database file whole groups of records can be selected according to a particular condition. This is known as a 'query'. Wessex Windows, for example, instruct their sales consultants to regularly select from the customer file all those customers who have a 'Yes' stored in the 'Further visit required' field.

■ Report files

It is possible to prepare special formats for printing part or all of the information in a database file on paper. Each special format may be saved in a file on disk, called a report. It is common to use several different reports with one database file, because one usually wants to view the same information on paper in a variety of ways.

■ Index files

In order to speed up the computer search through a database file for a particular record, or group of records, the user may give a command for the computer to create an index file. The index file will refer to one of the fields, and it can be thought of as being similar to the index in a text book – you look in the index for a particular word or phrase, the index gives the position of the references to that word or phrase, and so the reader can quickly find the information he or she is looking for. The index file on disk must be automatically updated by the computer when alterations are made to the file; (for example when new records are added, they must be added to the index file). The computer will do this without being prompted.

■ Program files

With most database programs it is possible to save a sequence of operations on a file which have to be frequently repeated in a special file called a program file.

John Snowdon has to make regular reports on the customers in his database, so that information can be used at head office. For one such report he has to sort the file into customer reference number order, then select only those customers who require a further visit, and print a list of the customers' details. This process would take several minutes for John to carry out, but he has stored the necessary commands in a special program file. He simply gives the name of this file and the computer does all the commands automatically.

Hardware for database

■ Processor

Any personal computer system is suitable for running a database program, but, as discussed previously, the more powerful the processor is the more efficiently the database will operate. For applications which require large files, storing hundreds or thousands of records, the more recent 486 or Pentium processor would be needed, otherwise the database will be too slow to use efficiently.

■ Monitor

There are no special requirements for a monitor, except that, if one of the later Windows-based database programs is used, quite high resolution is needed to obtain a clear image.

■ **Disk storage**

The disk storage available on the PC is critical for large files. Large files take up a lot of room, so this must be allowed for. However, just as important is the speed of operation of the hard disk drive – the faster the better as far as databases are concerned.

■ **Printer**

A problem which users encounter when printing the results of database work is the difficulty of fitting lists of records across a standard A4 sheet of paper. It is often impossible to do this, even if a small font size is selected, and so a wide carriage printer, which takes wider paper sizes, is recommended.

▶▶ **FIND OUT**

Find out about the printers available to you on your system, and whether a wide carriage printer may be used for printouts of lists from a database.

Activity 8.1 Employee file

SITUATION

You are to create a sample employee file for employees of Wessex Windows.

CONTENTS

Create database file structure; enter and edit records; save to disk and print to fit paper.

Level: INTERMEDIATE

Elements: PREPARE, PROCESS, PRESENT INFORMATION

TASKS

1 Run the database program on your system.

2 Create a new file to store the following information, where each record should store the information in one line of the table:

SURNAME	INITIALS	DEPT	SEX	GRADE
Green	F	Sales	M	1
Whyte	J G	Admin	M	1
Black	B	Sales	M	2
Browne	L D	Sales	F	2
Pinkerton	P	W/house	F	1
Redding	O	W/house	M	3
Gray	J	Marketing	F	3
Scarlet	K M B	Marketing	M	3

3 Save the file to your own disk or your own user area under the file name PERSONS1.

4 View the data one record at a time. Browse through the records in your database one by one from start to finish, to check that the data has been correctly entered. If there are any errors, change them by overtyping the information.

5 View the data in list form on the screen instead of one record on the screen at a time.

6 Insert the following new record into your database file (it does not matter whereabouts in the file it is inserted):

SURNAME	INITIALS	DEPT	SEX	GRADE
Purple	P	Sales	F	1

7 View the data one record at a time. Find the record for B Black, and change the Grade to Grade 3; he has been promoted.

8 Delete the record for J Gray; she has left the company.

9 Sort the records into order by the surname field.

10 Prepare a report to print the records showing the following fields (in this order) in columns on the printout:

| INITIALS | SURNAME | DEPT | GRADE | SEX |

Place the heading 'Personnel Report 1' at the top of the report. Place your own name at the bottom of the report.

11 Preview the printout, make any changes necessary to fit the printout on the paper (such as changing to a smaller font size if the printout is too wide). Obtain a printout.

12 Save the new version under the same file name (overwriting the previous file). Also make a back-up copy of the file under a different file name.

13 Print the records for these employees, using the same report (Report 1) as you used previously. In your own handwriting, neatly label the field type and size for each field shown on the printout.

14 List on screen, and then print on paper, the files in the current directory, including the file names for this activity.

15 Exit the database program.

Activity 8.2 Equipment database

SITUATION

You are to create a sample equipment file for record keeping at Wessex Windows.

CONTENTS

Create database file structure; enter and edit records; save to disk and print to fit paper.

Level: INTERMEDIATE

Elements: PREPARE, PROCESS, PRESENT INFORMATION

TASKS

1 Run the database program on your system.

2 Create a new file to store the following information, where each record should store the information in one line of the table.

EQUIPMENT	REFNUMBER	PRICE	DEPT
Photocopier	A103	1550	Admin
Laser printer	A432	950	Admin
Computer PC1	A651	800	Sales
Computer PC2	A109	800	W/house
Fax machine	A128	320	Admin
Modem	A332	260	Admin
Plotter	A401	475	Design
Scanner	A295	560	Design

3 Save the file to your own disk or your own user area under the file name EQUIP1.

4 View the data one record at a time. Browse through the records in your database one by one from start to finish, to check that the data has been correctly entered. If there are any errors, change them by overtyping the information.

5 View the data in list form on the screen instead of one record on the screen at a time.

6 Insert the following new record into your database file (it does not matter whereabouts in the file it is inserted):

EQUIPMENT	REFNUMBER	PRICE	DEPT
DM Printer	A328	200	Sales

7 View the data one record at a time. Find the record for the laser printer, and change the department to Design; it has been moved.

8 Delete the record for the modem; it has been written off and disposed of.

9 Sort the records into order by the EQUIPMENT field.

10 Prepare a report to print the records showing the following fields (in this order) in columns on the printout:

REFNUMBER	EQUIPMENT	DEPT	PRICE

Place the heading: 'Capital equipment: Report 1' at the top of the report. Place your own name at the bottom of the report.

11 Preview the printout, make any changes necessary to fit the printout on the paper (such as changing to a smaller font size if the printout is too wide). Obtain a printout.

12 Save the new version under the same file name (overwriting the previous file). Also make a back-up copy of the file under a different file name.

13 Print the records for these employees, using the same report (Report 1) as you used previously. In your own handwriting, neatly label the field type and size for each field shown on the printout.

14 List on screen, and then print on paper, the files in the current directory, including the file names for this activity.

15 Exit the database program.

Activity 8.3 Address book

SITUATION

You are required to develop a database file as a computerised address book. The file is to contain at least 15 records.

CONTENTS

Create database file; enter and edit data, save file to disk; sort records and select records according to given criteria; print reports to fit paper.

Levels: INTERMEDIATE, ADVANCED

Elements: PREPARE, PROCESS, PRESENT INFORMATION

TASKS

1 Run the database program.

2 You are to create a database file suitable for the storage of names and addresses of your friends, relatives and business contacts. Once the file has been created, the data can be entered. Remember to save the file regularly to floppy disk.

Each record is to contain the following fields:

- First name
- Surname
- Address line 1
- Address line 2
- Town/city
- County
- Post code
- Telephone number

Note that if this file were to be kept and updated for any length of time it would need to be registered under the Data Protection Act, as it contains personal data.

Create the database file by setting up each field in turn, using a suitable field name. Note that the field names do not have to appear exactly as above; in some database programs they will need to be abbreviated. Consult your program manual or lecturer/tutor for this information.

3 Add the following records to your database file:

Paul Henry
81 Desborough Road
Westleigh
S02 6QD
01703 456378

Graham Hodges
5 Kings Paddock
Summerslow
SALISBURY
SP5 1RZ
01722 411054

Felicity Knight
12 Greenwood Avenue
Southampton
SP2 4FS
01703 562321

Ian Wookey
45 Larkspur Gdns
Reading
Berks
RG5 4RT
01734 212234

Kenneth F West
Age 41, Male
5 Saracen Close
SALISBURY
Wilts
01722 322234

Bernadette Rees
Age 21, Female
7 Bison Walk
Andover
Hants
SP11 7NA
01704 569005

Ann Oxer
11 Catherine Close
Chandlers Ford
Hants
SO9 5BN
01705 221987

Note that some addresses contain more lines than others; some have a county and some do not. This should be dealt with by leaving the appropriate fields blank where necessary.

4 Add the details of at least 8 of your own friends, relatives or colleagues to the file. Save the file to your own floppy disk or your own user area under the file name PEOPLE1.

5 Print the entire file in the same order in which the data was entered. To do this you will probably need to create a report file (depending upon the database program you are using). The report file should be saved under a suitable file name, as it will be used again.

6 Sort the file into surname order.

7 Print the entire file in this order, using the same report as in task 5.

8 Select all the people who live in a certain town or city, for example Salisbury. Print the first name, surname and telephone number of these people using a new report file.

9 Select all people who live in a certain county, for example Hampshire, and print the complete record for each of these people using the report file created in task 5.

10 Now make the following changes to the appropriate records:

Graham Hodges does not live at 5 Kings Paddock; he lives at number 15.

Kenneth West's telephone number has changed; it is now 01722 437819

Ann Oxer has moved to:

Glebe Cottage
23 Stateside Crescent
Mickledown
Winchester
Hants
PS12 5TH
01562 110987

You may have to add an extra field to the record structure, because Ann Oxer's address is longer. Make the necessary changes.

Delete the record for Felicity Knight.

Make three other changes to the file for the records containing addresses of your own friends, relatives or colleagues.

11 Save the file under the same file name, overwriting the previous version. Make a back-up copy of the file under a different name and on a different drive or directory.

12 Print the entire file. In your own handwriting, neatly label the field type and size for each field shown on the printout.

13 List on screen, and then print on paper, the files in the current directory, including the file names for this activity.

14 Exit the database program.

Activity 8.4 Squash league database

SITUATION

You are required to develop a database file to store information on members of the Sportstown Leisure Centre squash league.

CONTENTS

Create database file; enter and edit data, save file to disk; sort records and select records according to given criteria; print reports to fit paper.

Levels: INTERMEDIATE, ADVANCED

Elements: PREPARE, PROCESS, PRESENT INFORMATION

TASKS

1 Run the database program.

2 Create a database file suitable for storing the following information:
- Surname
- First name
- Telephone number
- Current division
- Membership expiry date
- Points scored

3 Enter the following data to the database file:

John Davies
01722 435678
A
03/02/96
32

Peter Williams
01722 498698
B
23/09/96
18

Hazel Burridge
01722 768395
A
12/07/96
21

Len Parnell
01722 443567
D
21/12/95
33

John Farmer
01980 337650
D
20/01/96
32

Lesley Rudd
01980 233961
C
16/06/96
40

Database 157

Heather Partridge
01722 211398
A
30/01/96
11

Sheila Reddings
01722 443918
D
31/03/96
41

Patrick Herbertson
01980 997664
B
02/04/96
9

Kevin Strand
01703 219847
B
06/08/95
30

Brian Nillson
01980 213443
B
04/04/96
23

Howard Betts
01722 453900
C
08/12/95
28

John Wilson
01722 773625
C
29/11/96
33

Becky Downing
01703 211000
C
09/09/95
38

Damian Plockton
01980 710918
A
13/11/95
44

Susan Wilder
01722 232459
D
28/02/96
20

3 Ensure that the Membership expiry date field is set to store dates if this is possible in the database program which you are using.

4 Save the file to your own disk or your own user area under the file name LEAGUES1.

5 Print the complete file in the order in which the data was entered.

6 Sort the file into order by the surname field.

7 Print the Surname, First name and Division fields respectively.

8 Sort the file into order by the Division field so that the players in each of the four divisions are now grouped together.

9 Sort the file into order, first by Division, and secondly, by Points scored.

10 Save the new version under the same file name (overwriting the previous file). Also make a back-up copy of the file under a different file name.

11 Print the following fields from each record in the order of task 9: First name, Surname, Division, Points scored. Print the same information using a different layout. You may, for example, vary the heading, the column headings, the alignment, the font size or the paper orientation. Choose the most effective of the two layouts, and on the printout explain in your own handwriting why it is more effective.

12 List on screen, and then print on paper, the files in the current directory, including the file names for this activity.

13 Exit the database program.

Activity 8.5

SITUATION

Write a report on the advantages to Wessex Windows sales representatives of storing customer details on a computer database.

CONTENTS

Report on database advantages and potential security problems.

Levels: INTERMEDIATE, ADVANCED

Elements: EVALUATE THE USE OF I.T.

TASKS

1 Some sales representatives at Wessex Windows are using computers for much of their administrative work; others are not. Write a report to the Wessex Windows sales representatives on why they should consider storing all their customer details on a computer database.

2 In your report, which should be produced using a word processor, you should discuss the following:

- The advantages of using a database for this task instead of keeping manual (paper) records.
- Any disadvantages and potential pitfalls of using a database for this task.
- The facilities offered by the database which would not be possible with a manual system.
- How to keep the data safe and secure from loss or corruption.
- The importance of maintaining accuracy in such a database file.

3 The report should consist of between 500 and 750 words.

4 The report should be saved to disk and printed after careful checking.

Activity 8.6

SITUATION

Write a memorandum to all staff at Sportstown Leisure Centre on the advantages of storing their personnel details on a computer database.

CONTENTS

Report on database advantages and potential security and privacy problems.

Level: ADVANCED

Elements: EVALUATE THE USE OF I.T.

TASKS

1. Some staff at the leisure centre are concerned about the computer system being used to keep personnel records (in a database). Until recently, these records have been kept in a manual filing system, and you are required to explain the advantages and disadvantages of computerisation for this personnel records system. Write a memorandum to all staff explaining the issues. Refer to Chapters 8 (Database), 12 (People and computers) and 13 (Hardware for information technology) in order to research this issue.

2. In your memo, which should be produced using a word processor, you should discuss the following:

    - The advantages of using a database for this task instead of keeping manual (paper) records, in terms of speed, ease of use, accuracy and security.
    - Any disadvantages and potential pitfalls of using a database for this task.
    - The facilities offered by the database which would not be possible with a manual system.
    - How to keep the data safe and secure from loss or corruption.
    - How to keep the data private.
    - The implications of the Data Protection Act for this task.
    - The importance of maintaining accuracy in such a database file.

3. The memorandum should consist of between 500 and 750 words.

4. The report should be saved to disk and printed after careful checking.

Activity 8.7 Holiday Cottages Database

SITUATION

Create and use a database file for storing details of country holiday cottages.

CONTENTS

Create database file; enter and edit data, save file to disk; sort records and select records according to given criteria; print reports to fit paper.

Level: ADVANCED

Elements: PREPARE, PROCESS, PRESENT INFORMATION

TASKS

1 Run the database program on your system.

2 Create a file suitable for storing the information listed below, and then enter the information itself:

Reference	NF102
Location	RINGWOOD
Description	Beautiful 18th-century gamekeeper's cottage
Beds	2
Sleeps	4
Garden	Y
Price code	C

Reference	NF101
Location	BOURNEMOUTH
Description	3 bedroom detached house in non-estate location
Beds	3
Sleeps	6
Garden	Y
Price code	F

Reference	CW53
Location	ST IVES
Description	Attractive seaside location
Beds	2
Sleeps	5
Garden	N
Price code	G

Reference	NW23
Location	BARMOUTH
Description	Cliff-top cottage with views over the bay
Beds	4
Sleeps	10
Garden	Y
Price code	L

Reference	SC04
Location	GLENELG
Description	Fisherman's cottage near the village
Beds	2
Sleeps	5
Garden	Y
Price code	D

Reference	SC21
Location	SKYE
Description	Modern bungalow overlooking the Sound of Sleat
Beds	3
Sleeps	5
Garden	N
Price code	G

Reference	KT33
Location	BROADSTAIRS
Description	Family house in quiet position
Beds	3
Sleeps	7
Garden	Y
Price code	J

Reference	KT34
Location	MARGATE
Description	Modernised 17th-century town house
Beds	2
Sleeps	4
Garden	N
Price code	G

Reference	KT42
Location	FOLKESTONE
Description	Modernised Victorian terrace on the sea front
Beds	2
Sleeps	4
Garden	Y
Price code	G

Reference	NW37
Location	PORTHMADOG
Description	Attractive town centre position
Beds	4
Sleeps	12
Garden	Y
Price code	L

3 Save the file to your own disk or your own user area under the file name COTTS1.

4 Prepare a report in order to print out certain parts (fields) of each selected record in the database. This report (Report 1) should tell the computer to print the Reference, Location and Price code of each record.

5 Preview the printout of the records for Report 1, make any adjustments necessary to fit the information on the page, then print the report.

6 Sort the records into order by Price code, cheapest first. (Price code A would be the cheapest.)

7 Print the selected records in this order using Report 1.

8 Sort the records into order by the Reference field (from A to Z). Prepare a new report (Report 2) which shows the Reference, Location,

Sleeps and Price code fields. Keeping the records in the same order, print Report 2 (having previewed and adjusted where necessary first).

9 Construct a query to select all cottages which have a garden. Display these on the screen and show your lecturer/tutor for checking.

10 Construct a query to select all cottages which sleep 5 or more and have a garden. Display the Reference, Location and Price code on the screen and show your lecturer/tutor for checking.

11 Make a back-up copy of the file under a different name and on a different drive or directory.

12 Use Report 1 to print the Reference, Location and Price code on paper, having previewed and adjusted where necessary first. Print the same information using a different layout. You may, for example, vary the heading, the column headings, the alignment, the font size or the paper orientation. Choose the most effective of the two layouts, and on the printout explain in your own handwriting why it is more effective. Also neatly label the field type and size for each field shown on the printouts.

13 Write a short report (200 to 300 words) on the advantages and disadvantages (to both the company and the customer) of using a computerised database system to store the holiday cottage details, rather than a manual storage system.

14 List on screen, and then print on paper, the files in the current directory, including the file names for this activity.

15 Exit the database program.

Activity 8.8 Cars database

SITUATION

You are required to develop a database of cars for sale.

CONTENTS

Collect data and choose file structure for a database file; enter and edit data, save file to disk; sort records and select records according to given criteria; print reports to fit paper.

Level: ADVANCED

Elements: PREPARE, PROCESS, PRESENT INFORMATION
EVALUATE THE USE OF I.T.

TASKS

1 Collect car sales data from a local newspaper or similar source. Run the database program on your system. Create a file and enter some of the data (at least 15 records) from the car sales details. Choose the fields carefully, so that it is possible to carry out the searches and sorts listed in the questions that follow.

2 Sort by registration letter, newest first.

3 Sort by make and print all details. You may need to adjust the font size and report column widths in order to obtain a compact printout.

4 Sort by make as the first field, then model.

5 Select all of one make and print reg. letter, make, model and colour.

6 Select all blue cars and print make and model.

7 Select commercial vehicles and print make, model and reg. letter.

8 Sort the file into order so that the makes are listed alphabetically, and within makes the models are listed in age order, newest first.

9 Obtain 5 extra car details and add them to the file.

10 Delete three records of cars which have been sold.

11 Save this second version of the file under a suitable file name (keeping the first version). Make a back-up copy of the file under a different name and on a different drive or directory.

12 Print the file in the same order as for task 8. In your own handwriting, neatly label the field type and size for each field shown on the printout.

13 Write a short report (200 to 300 words) on the advantages and disadvantages (to both a car dealer and to one of its customers) of using a computerised database system to store the car details, rather than a manual storage system.

14 List on screen, and then print on paper, the files in the current directory, including the file names for this activity.

15 Exit the database program.

9 Communications

Background to communications

Computer systems are used not only to process, store and present information, but also to communicate that information to other computer users. The technological changes which are going on in modern societies probably mean that computers will be the central feature of most means of communicating.

Communication between computers has become as important to businesses and individuals as the actual processing which the computer system carries out. Some aspects of communications which are carried out with the aid of computers are:

- The transmission of simple word-processed documents between users inside an organisation.
- The transmission of word-processed documents or other messages between one organisation and another.
- The transmission of more complex documents (such as desktop published documents containing images) from suppliers to customers.
- The retrieval of items of information from a large database which may be at a great distance from the user who is searching for the information.
- Ordering goods from a supplier.
- Carrying out banking or other financial operations from home or office, such as requesting bank statements or making payments from a bank account.
- The use of an electronic mail system to send receive, store and reply to

messages; this may be done internally through a local area network of personal computers, or via a national or international electronic mail system.

- The booking by travel agents of individual holidays and aircraft seats.

Modem communications

A PC can communicate with another computer system by using a telephone network as the channel along which the message is transmitted. To do this, the user needs a modem attached to his or her PC. The modem converts the digital signals of the PC into a form suitable for sending along telephone cables, and converts the signals back to digital form when the signal is received.

Fig. 14 Modem

■ The choice of modem

In order for a communications system between computers through telephone networks to work efficiently, the modem needs to be fast enough at converting and sending its data so that the user does not have to wait too long for a response to his or her enquiries. In addition, there has to be quite a sophisticated level of error checking. Error checking and correction is vital in communications due to the nature of telephone lines. These lines, especially where they are the older analogue lines, suffer from noise: that is, random electrical signals which, particularly over longer distances can blot out parts of the signals travelling along the lines.

Error checking and correction is a feature of some, but certainly not all modems for PCs. The error correction can be built into the modem in the form of hardware, or it can be a part of the communications software being used, or more often, both. As a general rule, the faster you attempt to send data along a telephone line the more errors due to noise will be noticed, and so messages which have to be 100 per cent correct on receipt must be sent more slowly.

A more expensive modem will send data at high speed and will include enough error checking and correction to be able to cope with the speed. Of course, an important factor for both the business and the home user is that the slower the signals are sent and received, the more time will be spent on line, and so the higher will be the cost of the telephone call. Add to this on-line charges for the email system being used or the database being accessed and the total cost can be rather high. To summarise, then, the higher specification modems which are available will give a better and, in the long run, a cheaper service to the communication user.

Bulletin boards

Many bulletin boards are in existence at any time, some operated by groups of home users, some operated for profit, and yet others run by companies to provide a service to employees or customers. These bulletin boards can generally offer any of the following:

- Thousands of files available on-line for downloading; many of these are shareware program files: that is, programs which can be tried out first and then if the user wants to continue to use the program pay a registration fee.
- Public domain files, which are free to the user who chooses to download them.
- Conferencing systems, where users can join in a computerised conference.

■ **Conferencing systems**

In a computerised conference, the user can read the contributions which have been made to the conference by other users, and add their own points. Examples of conferencing systems are Cosy, on the CIX (Compulink Information Exchange) service, and Caucus on the education-oriented Campus 2000 service. The subjects which are discussed in these conferences may be computer-based, or they can be of general interest. With some systems the ordinary user can start their own conference; they act as the 'moderator' or organiser of the conference. The claimed advantages of conferencing systems are as follows:

- People may contribute to a conference any time and from anywhere (as long as they have a computer, modem and telephone socket).
- Participants in a computerised conference do not feel embarrassed about making points at the conference as they may at a real conference (in fact they may make more sensible contributions, since they will read other contributions and have time to plan their own points properly).
- There are no travelling or accommodation costs as there are for a real, face-to-face conference.

Electronic mail (Email) on BT's 'Telecom Gold'

This is a subset of the Telecom Gold messaging service, and it enables users to leave messages for other users in 'electronic pigeon-holes'. In fact these pigeon-holes are really areas of storage on a central computer; each user is allocated such a storage area for his or her mail. When the user requests it, he or she is shown the messages which have been sent by other users. This kind of system can be used in quite a sophisticated way. The features available on email systems include the following:

■ **Send a message to an individual user**

You give the user's 'address', which enables the computer and network system to leave the message you write in the user's pigeon-hole. When the user next logs into the mail system, he or she is told that there is a message waiting to be read. Generally, the user is asked to enter a short summary of the message called the 'subject'. This is seen by the recipient

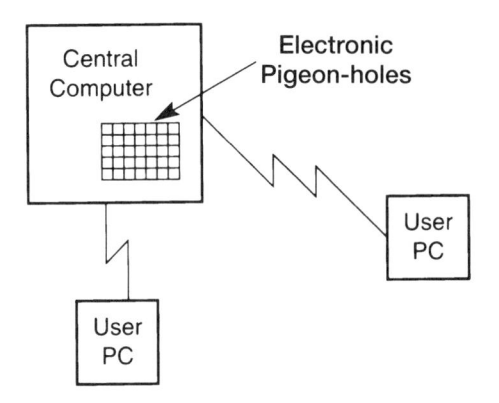

Fig. 15 Email system

when he or she scans his mail. For example, he or she may have 15 items of mail in the mailbox. Rather than reading through the complete message of each one in turn, he or she scans the subjects to see a summary of the contents of the messages.

When the subject has been typed, the main body of the message itself is entered, and there will be a specific method of ending the message, for example to put a full stop as the only character on a new line. Usually it is possible to edit the message in case any changes are required before it is finally sent.

■ Send a message to a mailing list

All email systems allow the user to construct mailing lists. These are lists of the user names of other users of the email system. A message can then be sent to all the users on the mailing list rather than just one user. In this way one can send notice of a meeting, for example to all the members of a committee.

■ Request acknowledgement

It is often useful to find out whether users have read the message you sent to them, whether this be an individual or a group of users on a mailing list. This can be done by requesting an acknowledgement when you send a message. When the user reads his or her message the computer system places a note to tell you this in your own mailbox.

- **Send prepared messages**

    For longer messages – for example documents of several pages rather than short notes – you may want to use a word processor for preparation of your documents rather than the message creation and editing feature of the email system itself. This feature is available on many email systems; the way to use it is to prepare your document in the usual way, save it as a disk file, then log into the email system and give the instruction to send the mail message from the file.

- **Scan and read messages**

    Normally the routine when logging into your mailbox is to check for any new messages which have been left for you by other users. The messages can either be read while on line, or saved to disk and read later, or printed to read later. When a message has been read, there is an opportunity to reply to it immediately. (The system will know what address to send the reply to.) If a message has been read and is no longer needed it can be deleted.

- **Forward mail**

    Some messages are for reading and then sending on to another user. This can generally be done, and you may wish to amend or add to the message before forwarding it.

- **Send files by email**

    From time to time the you might want to send files, such as program files, image files, spreadsheet files, and so on, rather than simple text files. This is often available on email systems, but you must be careful to use the right file protocol. A protocol is simply a format for sending files between computer that is agreed by the sending and receiving computers. The protocol is important for these files, since any errors in a transmitted program file, for example, would make the file useless. In contrast, it probably does not matter if the odd few characters in a text message have been corrupted in the transmission process.

    Common protocols for sending and receiving such files are Kermit, Xmodem and Zmodem. The differences between them amount to varying speeds of transmission and methods of data checking and correction.

The Internet

The Internet (sometimes called the information superhighway) is a world-wide network of computer systems. All kinds of computers can be connected to the Internet, and the physical link between them can be telephone cables, satellite connections, optical fibre or other types of cable.

No one organisation or person 'controls' the Internet, but it exists on the basis of an agreed set of procedures for establishing connections between computer systems.

Every computer on the Internet has an unique address, just as an individual household has an address. By using these addresses, one can establish a link to a computer anywhere in the world, as long as it is on the Internet. This can be used to transfer files, pictures, software and other information.

Electronic mail messages can be sent over the Internet, and currently this is probably the cheapest, fastest and most reliable way of communicating over long distances. It only works, however, if the person or organisation that you are communicating with has an Internet address. The Internet is growing very quickly, as more businesses and individuals realise that this is a cheap and efficient means of communication. Microsoft's PC operating system, Windows 95, includes software to allow access to the Internet.

Making a connection to the Internet can be complex, unless the communications software you are using has already been correctly set up. The most user-friendly way of accessing the Internet is to use a feature called the World Wide Web. This allows the transfer of images as well as text and is designed to allow the user to browse through information, clicking the mouse on a word or image to obtain further information.

Activity 9.1 Electronic mail 1

SITUATION

Use an electronic mail system for sending and receiving simple messages. You are to send a short message to another user of the email system. The other user should have his or her own mailbox. Wait for a reply to your message; when the reply has been received, send the other user some more detailed information.

CONTENTS

Log onto a secure system. Use electronic mail for sending and receiving simple messages.

Levels: INTERMEDIATE, ADVANCED

Elements: PREPARE, PROCESS INFORMATION

TASKS

1. Run the electronic mail (EMAIL) program on your system.

2. Log into your mailbox, using the correct user name together with the matching password. Note that if you do not have these items of information you will not be able to use the system.

3. Send the following message to the other user. For this you need to know the user name (mailbox number) of the other user.

   Subject:

   IT User Group

   Message:

   There will be a meeting of the Information Technology User Group on Monday 10 June 1996.

   The meeting will take place in Room 25A, from 2.00 to 3.30pm.

   Please acknowledge receipt of this message and let me know whether you can attend.

   Regards

   IT User Group Chairman

4. Log out from the EMAIL program.

5. Allow sufficient time for the other email user to read this message and reply to it.

6. While you are waiting for the reply, prepare the following detailed

information, ready to go out to the same user once the reply has been received. Depending upon your particular system you may either prepare the message in your normal word processor program, or it may be preferable to use the EMAIL program itself.

Subject:

User Group agenda

Message:

IT USER GROUP

Notice of Meeting
Monday 10 June 1996
2.00–3.30pm
Conference Room 25A

AGENDA

1   Apologies for absence
2   Minutes of the last meeting
3   Matters arising
4   Discussion: the IT budget for 1997. Members are requested to put forward their spending proposals
5   IT Manager's report
6   Any other business

The meeting will close by 3.30pm.

7 Print a copy of the agenda from the EMAIL program. In your own handwriting, neatly label the places in the document where you used tabs or formatting (such as underline, bold, italic, etc.) to improve the layout of the document.

8 Save the email agenda to your own disk or your own user area under the file name ITAGENDA. Also make a back-up copy of the file under a different file name.

9 Log into the EMAIL program read your mail, and if the other user has replied, send the previously prepared message to him or her.

10 List on screen, and then print on paper, the files in the current directory, including the file names for this activity.

11 Exit the EMAIL program.

Activity 9.2 Electronic mail 2

SITUATION

Use an electronic mail system for sending and receiving simple messages. You are to send a short message to another user of the email system. The other user should have his or her own mailbox. Wait for a reply to your message; when the reply has been received, send the other user some more detailed information.

CONTENTS

Log onto a secure system; use electronic mail for sending and receiving simple messages.

Levels: INTERMEDIATE, ADVANCED

Elements: PREPARE, PROCESS, PRESENT INFORMATION

TASKS

1 Run the electronic mail (EMAIL) program on your system.

2 Log into your mailbox, using the correct user name together with the matching password. Note that if you do not have these items of information you will not be able to use the system.

3 Send the following message to the other user. For this you need to know the user name (mailbox number) of the other user.

Subject:

Surveyors' course

Message:

There are a number of places available on the Surveyors' course, which takes place the week after next. Please let me know if you are interested in attending. The course lasts for five days.

Regards
Area Sales Manager

4 Log out from the EMAIL program.

5 Allow sufficient time for the other email user to read this message and reply to it.

6 While you are waiting for the reply, prepare the following detailed information, ready to go out to the same user once the reply has been received. Depending upon your particular system you may either prepare the message in your normal word processor program, or it may be preferable to use the EMAIL program itself. Make two copies of the message in case of accidental loss.

Subject:

Surveyors' course details

Message:

WESSEX WINDOWS
SURVEYORS' TRAINING COURSE

The Ship Hotel
Clearbridge
Monday 16 May to Friday 24 May 1996

COURSE CONTENT:

Monday am:	Introductions and overview
pm:	The new product range
Tuesday:	The manufacturing specifications
Wednesday and Thursday:	Practical instructions and seminars
Friday:	Using the new PC software for manufacture instructions

The cost of the course is £750 to invited employees of Wessex Windows. This will be deducted from commissions where there is an agreement to do so in the employee's contract; otherwise it will need to be paid in advance.

The cost is fully inclusive of accommodation, breakfast and evening meals.

7 Print a copy of the agenda from the EMAIL program. In your own handwriting, neatly label the places in the document where you used tabs or formatting (such as underline, bold, italic, etc.) to improve the layout of the document.

8 Save the email agenda to your own disk or your own user area under the file name WWCOURSE. Also make a back-up copy of the file under a different file name.

9 List on screen, and then print on paper, the files in the current directory, including the file names for this activity.

11 Exit the EMAIL program.

Activity 9.3 Bulletin Boards

SITUATION

Set up a communications program to dial and communicate with a bulletin board.

CONTENTS

Set communications parameters to enable communication with a remote computer; log onto a secure system; receive and transmit files in a format to ensure successful transmission.

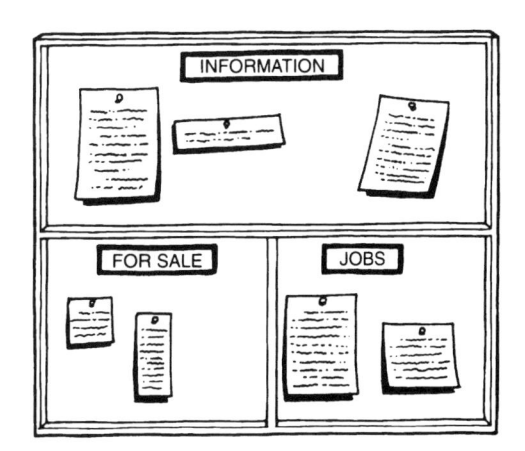

Communications **179**

Levels: INTERMEDIATE, ADVANCED

Elements: PROCESS INFORMATION
EVALUATE THE USE OF I.T.

PREPARATION

Prepare for this activity by looking up (with the help of your lecturer/tutor if needed) the telephone numbers and other details of two bulletin boards. These should be as close to you as possible, since the telephone charges will be cheaper. It is possible to find advertisements for bulletin boards in most personal computer magazines. Most advertisements for bulletin boards give the location of the computer which you will be dialling up. Be sure to pick a bulletin board which uses normal rate telephone lines; a few use premium rate lines, and these would be very expensive.

TASKS

1 Run the communications program on your system. Ensure that your communications program is properly set up, in particular with the following information:

- the port the modem is connected to (COM1, COM2, COM3 or COM4);
- the terminal emulation to use (see your modem manual for this).

It may well be that these items of information are already set up for you.

2 Create a new service in your communications program.

3 Set up the information which the computer needs for the new service. You will need to type in the following details:

- the name of the bulletin board;
- the telephone number;
- the baud rate (depends partly on the maximum baud rate of the modem you are using);
- the number of data bits;
- the number of stop bits;
- whether full duplex or half duplex.

Most bulletin boards operate on no parity, 8 data bits, 1 stop bit and full duplex. The baud rate you use depends partly on your modem and also on the rate offered by the bulletin board.

4 When you have entered all the settings for the bulletin board, the service should be saved. The method of saving depends on your communications program.

5 Dial the number for the service you have set up.

6 When the computer which runs the bulletin board answers, you will be asked to identify yourself, and possibly to specify a password to use on future occasions when you contact the board. Make sure the password you use is one that you will remember.

7 Some bulletin boards are free; others charge a subscription; but most will allow you to make use of the service for long enough to carry out this activity.

8 Follow the instructions on the screen. Look for the features offered by the bulletin board, such as email and downloading and uploading of files. When you have investigated the menu systems, log off from this bulletin board.

9 Try the same with another bulletin board. This time try to download a file. This means that a file will be transferred from the computer system of the bulletin board, through the telephone line and into your computer system, where it will be stored on your hard disk. Do not choose a large file, as this may take a long time to be transferred, incurring high telephone charges. (The bulletin board will tell you the approximate length of time it will take to download the file.) The files available are generally shareware or public domain software, both of which are free until and if you decide to keep using the software, at which point you may have to pay to register your copy.

10 If you make further use of a bulletin board, you should also upload some files. This means that you send a file from your computer through the telephone line to the bulletin board computer, where, if it is suitable, it will be made available to other users of the system. (Some bulletin boards will not let you continue to download files until you have also uploaded some.)

11 Try to find out what service this board offers, and compare it to the first one you tried. When you have finished, ensure that you log off from the bulletin board correctly; if you do not, the line may become unavailable to other users for a time. (Follow the instructions on the screen for logging off.)

12 Your lecturer/tutor should check that you have successfully accessed these bulletin boards.

13 Exit from the communications program.

Activity 9.4 Conferencing systems

SITUATION

Communicate with a bulletin board, and participate in a conferencing system on the bulletin board.

CONTENTS

Communicate with a remote computer. Log onto a secure system. Apply search routines. Save messages to disk and print messages.

Level: ADVANCED
Elements: PROCESS INFORMATION
EVALUATE THE USE OF I.T.

TASKS

1 Run the communications program on your system.

2 Call up a bulletin board or information service which offers a conferencing system. You will need to give the correct user name and password, so that the host computer recognises you as a valid user.

3 List the conferences (some or all of them) which are available on the system. Note which ones are open conferences (open to any user) or closed (for all except invited users).

4 Join a conference which you think may interest you. Conferences are usually separated into different subjects; for example, there may be a conference on personal computers, and another one on environmental issues.

5 Read some of the contributions which have been made by other members of the conference. These may be read in a particular order, or you may be able to view only the contributions made after a particular date.

6 Send (at least) two contributions direct to a printer. Save two contributions to a disk file. Remember to load these into a word processor to read them when you are off line from the conferencing system.

7 Make your own contribution to the conference as a response to some of the ideas you have read about in the conference so far.

8 Leave the conference, log off from the bulletin board or other information service.

9 Exit the communications program.

Activity 9.5 Electronic Mail 3

SITUATION

Use an electronic mail system for sending and receiving messages. Messages to be prepared off line in a word processor. Messages to be sent to a mailing list.

CONTENTS

Log onto a secure system; use electronic mail for sending and receiving messages; files prepared off line to be sent to multiple destinations; save files in specific formats and under variety of file names.

Level: ADVANCED
Elements: PREPARE, PROCESS, PRESENT INFORMATION

TASKS

1 Run the word processor program on your system.

2 Create a new document and enter the following text.

Subject:

IT User Group Exhibition

Message:

I have provisionally arranged for a number of computer software companies to come to the Leisure Centre on Thursday 6 April 1995 to show us their programs for sports bookings. As you know, the current computer bookings system needs improving, and we discussed at our last user group meeting the possibility of staff who use the system viewing alternatives.

I am not sure if the arrangements will suit, or whether there are any other plans for that day. If there is a problem, the date can be changed, as it is a long time ahead.

Please let me know what you think.

Thanks!
Alan.

Do not change the layout of the text, as it will be saved as a text file. (A text file stores only the text and new line characters, not the precise layout.)

3 Use the spell check to find and correct any mistakes in the text, and do an on-screen check also.

4 The file is now to be saved as a text (or DOS) file. This will be an option within the saving routine on your word processor program. Save the file to your own disk or your own user area as a text (or DOS) file, under the file name MAILDOC1.

5 Exit the word processor.

6 Run the EMAIL program on your system. Log in under your user name and give the correct password when requested.

7 Choose another user of the EMAIL system to send the document MAILDOC1 to. Generally this will be done by sending a message to the other user, and attaching a DOS or text file to the message. You will need to give the file name MAILDOC1 so that the EMAIL program can find the message to send.

8 Exit the EMAIL program.

9 Run the word processor program on your system, and create a new file for the following text, which is also to be stored as a text (or DOS) file, but this time under the file name MAILDOC2.

Attention all staff

A small exhibition of software for personal computers is to be held in the main hall of the centre on Thursday 6 April. There will be a variety of software programs to view and try out, but the particular emphasis will be on selecting a new 'activities booking program' for the centre's computer system.

This small exhibition has been organised by the IT User Group, and we hope that all staff will come along and actually try out the software. Make any comments and recommendations you have regarding the software to the centre manager afterwards.

10 Make a back-up copy of the file under a different file name.

11 Exit the word processor program and run the EMAIL program, logging in under your usual user name and password.

12 Prepare a mailing list of at least three other users of the EMAIL system. If possible, name the mailing list MEMBERS.

13 Send the document MAILDOC2 to the mailing list MEMBERS.

14 Print a copy of MAILDOC2. In your own handwriting, neatly label the places in the document where you used the return or tab key.

15 List on screen, and then print on paper, the files in the current directory, including the file names for this activity.

16 When you have sent the message to the mailing list, check that the documents in this activity have been received, then clear your mailbox of any unwanted messages.

17 Exit the EMAIL program.

10 Charts

Background to charts

A business graphics program will enable you to produce a wide variety of graphs and charts. A well-known program of this type is Harvard Graphics, and it is this program which we will concentrate on in this chapter. Other, similar programs may be used for the same activities. The typical range of charts available includes:

- Line chart
- Bar chart
- Pie chart
- Text chart
- Area chart
- Scatter chart
- High/low/close chart
- Organisation chart

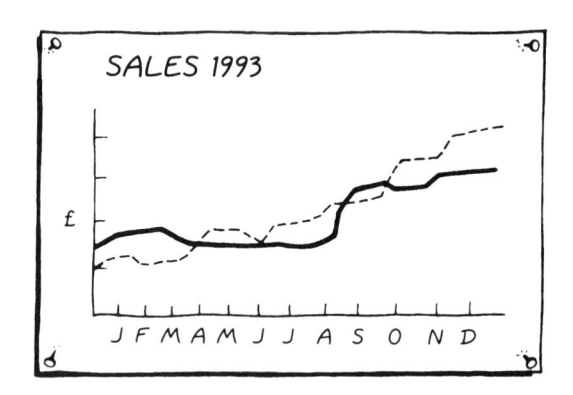

■ Drawings

In addition, you can add drawings and symbols to your charts. The drawings may be created in Harvard Graphics, or can be imported from other software. Symbol files are provided with the main program, and the user can select symbols to add to his or her charts from these libraries of files.

An alternative to using a specialist program designed specifically for the production of charts is to use the chart drawing feature of a spreadsheet program. Most spreadsheets have this facility, but some offer better quality charts than others. The chart feature in some spreadsheet programs is fairly limited, and not as flexible as the facility in a program like Harvard Graphics.

If you are reviewing a program, to check whether the chart facility is what you need, these are some of the points to look for:

- Can you draw simple line, pie and bar charts?
- Can you change the chart type easily, while working with a fixed set of data ? This is a frequent requirement, because the user may want to enter the numerical data first, then use the software to show what the data would look like with a range of different chart types.
- Will the software accept several sets of data for one chart, to produce what are called multiple or compound charts? Is it possible to combine different charts on one chart, for example to display one series of numbers as bars and a second series as a line?
- Can the scale on each axis of the chart be varied, or does the user have to accept the program's decision on the scale?
- Are special effects available in the charting facility; for example: to change the colouring of the bars in a bar chart; to display a pie chart in 3-dimensional form; or to choose from a range of different symbols for display of the points in a scatter diagram?

Software for charts

➤➤ **FIND OUT**

Find out what software you are to use for drawing charts. Find out also how to run the program on your system.

A charting program is an applications program offered on personal computers which can save the user a lot of time, and can produce very fast results. The usual business requirement for charting is to start with a set of numerical data which is to be displayed in the form of charts. The reason for this is to add clarity to a presentation; people find it easier in general to understand numerical information if it is shown as charts.

To draw a series of charts by hand would take considerable time; first, the numbers may have to be analysed (e.g. turned into percentages of a total), then the charts must be drawn. The computer running a charting program is doing all the calculations required.

In addition, the computer offers the user a choice of a number of chart types; the user merely enters the numbers and then the different types can be tried out on the screen and the most suitable one chosen.

■ Simple charts

The range of different chart types offered has been discussed above, and you must check to find out what is offered in the program which you are using. Most people understand what is meant by bar, line and pie charts. A high/low close chart is used for displaying the progress of share prices or similar products which have a changing value over a period of time. For example, the chart enables you to record, for share prices, the highest and lowest value of a share each day and the opening and closing values of the share each day over a number of days.

■ Scatter chart

A scatter chart shows the relationship between two variables. For example, one could display, for a number of companies, their expenditure on advertising as one variable and their sales as the other. Plotting a point for each pair of values for a number of different companies would indicate on the scatter diagram whether there is a link between the amount of advertising a company does and the value of its sales. If the relationship was a strong one, this would show on the scatter diagram because the plotted points would be near to a single straight line.

■ Organisation chart

An organisation chart is used to show in the form of a diagram the structure of a company or other organisation. Each person or role in the organisation is placed in a box, and the boxes are linked together on different levels by lines for a hierarchical tree structure. The chart can show who reports to whom in a company, and what functional areas in the company are the responsibility of which people. As with the other charts offered in the software, it should be possible to vary the style of the chart, which in the case of organisation charts would largely consist of changing the sizes of the lettering and the boxes.

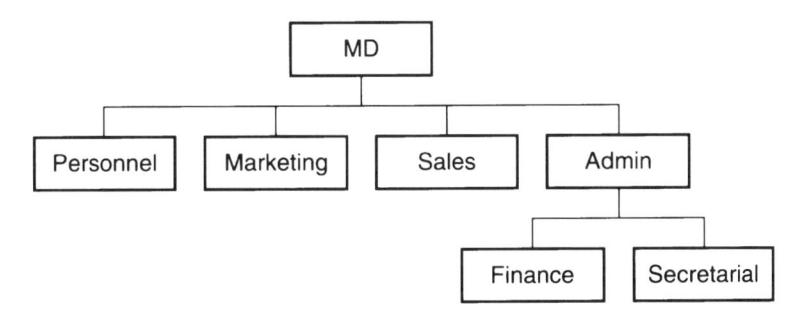

Fig. 16 Organisation chart

Hardware for chart drawing

■ Processor

A standard PC is suitable for chart drawing, but, as is the case with most programs which place a lot of importance on the visual appearance of the end product, the processor will be doing a lot of work and therefore needs to be fairly fast. This means that the processor in the PC should be a 386 or later. An earlier processor would be incapable of generating the screen display fast enough (with recent software) to make the program efficient to use.

■ Monitor

A colour monitor is needed to take advantage of the colour features offered in chart drawing software. Even if the finished graph is to be output to a black and white printer, the user will still find a colour monitor much easier to work with. The reason is that the software has been designed to work with a colour monitor.

■ Disk storage

Standard disk storage is acceptable; the data files created as the software is being used are not especially large. However, the chart drawing program will be making frequent accesses to the disk while the program is in use; every time you change an element of the chart on the screen, the data stored in the RAM or on disk must be updated, and so a fast disk drive will speed up operation of the program.

■ **Printer**

A good printer is essential to successful use of a chart drawing program. Clearly, the chart produced is only as good as the printer which prints it out, although in some cases it is the screen image of the chart which is the final product. A dot matrix printer can print charts, but they will be of low quality, since a dot matrix printer is primarily designed for the printing of text. A laser printer is ideal; colour if possible.

Activity 10.1

SITUATION

Draw a stacked bar chart.

CONTENTS

Enter data to specific chart type; add labels; save to disk and print; include chart in memorandum.

Level: INTERMEDIATE

Elements: PREPARE, PRESENT INFORMATION

TASKS

1 Run the graph drawing program.

2 Draw a line graph of the following data:

Sales 1995 (£m)

JAN	FEB	MAR	APR	MAY	JUN
23	17	20	21	22	22

JUL	AUG	SEP	OCT	NOV	DEC
19	23	24	27	26	28

3 Place an appropriate title on the graph.

4 Save the graph to your own disk or your own user area under the file name GRAPH1, and then print it.

5 Using the same data, convert the graph to a bar chart, save it under the file name GRAPH2, and print it.

6 Draw a pie chart of the following data:

Sales (1995) – by region (£m)

N.EAST	N.WEST	WALES	MIDLANDS	SOUTH
21	34	43	42	44

7 Place an appropriate title on the graph.

8 Save the graph to your own disk or your own user area under the file name GRAPH3, and then print it.

9 Draw a stacked bar chart for the following data:

Sales (1995) – by region and product (£m)

	N.EAST	N.WEST	WALES	MIDLANDS
Spirits	11	20	21	20
Wine	6	8	9	9
Beer	4	6	12	13

10 Place an appropriate title on the graph.

11 Save the chart to your own disk or your own user area under the file name GRAPH4. Also make a back-up copy of the file under a different file name.

12 Ensure that the values you entered are displayed on the chart. Print the final version of the chart. In your own handwriting, neatly label the values entered on the printout.

13 List on screen, and then print on paper, the files in the current directory, including the file names for this activity.

14 Exit from the graph program.

15 You must now include your chart in a memorandum. Use a word processor program to prepare the heading and introduction for this memorandum. The introduction should describe the information which the chart shows.

16 Use cut and paste (or a similar technique, depending on the software you are using), to transfer the chart to the memorandum. You may need to make adjustments to the layout in order to fit the chart on the page. Add your own short commentary, describing briefly the main features of the information shown in the chart.

17 Save the memorandum, preview and then obtain a printout.

18 Exit the word processor program.

Activity 10.2

SITUATION

You have been given the task of analysing and presenting some statistical information on the use of various sporting activities at Sportstown Leisure Centre. The Centre Manager has told you that it is important that the tables and charts you produce are clear, attractive and well labelled.

CONTENTS

Enter data to specific chart type; add labels; save to disk and print; include chart in memorandum.

Level: INTERMEDIATE
Elements: PREPARE, PRESENT INFORMATION

TASKS

1 Run the chart drawing program.

2 Enter the following data into the program to produce a simple vertical bar chart:

Sportstown Leisure Centre

Squash sessions sold: January–June 1995

Jan	Feb	Mar	Apr	May	Jun
743	789	806	853	740	661

Ensure that the two title lines shown above appear on the chart.

On the vertical axis, put the axis label '**Sessions**'.

On the horizontal axis, put the axis label '**Month**'.

3 Save the chart to your own disk or your own user area under the file name SQCHT1.

4 Preview the printout of the chart. Check that the appearance is satisfactory, and that the position on the paper will be suitable, then print the chart.

5 An error in the data has been found. The figure for March should have been 906. Make this change to the chart and save again under the same file name (overwriting the previous version). Make a back-up copy of the file under a different file name.

6 Ensure that the values you entered are displayed on the graph. Print the final version of the chart. In your own handwriting, neatly label the values entered on the printout.

7 List on screen, and then print on paper, the files in the current directory, including the file names for this activity.

8 Exit the chart drawing program.

9 You must now include your chart in a memorandum. Use a word processor program to prepare the heading and introduction for this memorandum. The introduction should describe the information which the chart shows.

10 Use cut and paste (or a similar technique, depending on the software you are using), to transfer the chart to the memorandum. You may need to make adjustments to the layout in order to fit the chart on the page. Add your own short commentary, describing briefly the main features of the information shown in the chart.

11 Save the memorandum, preview and then obtain a printout.

12 Exit the word processor program.

Activity 10.3

SITUATION

You have been given the task of analysing and presenting some statistical information on the use of various sporting activities at Sportstown Leisure Centre. The Centre Manager has told you that it is important that the tables and charts you produce are clear, attractive and well labelled.

CONTENTS

Enter data to specific chart type; add labels; save to disk and print; include chart in memorandum.

Level: INTERMEDIATE
Elements: PREPARE, PRESENT INFORMATION

TASKS

1 Run the chart drawing program.

2 Enter the following data into the program to produce a simple vertical bar chart:

Sportstown Leisure Centre

Table tennis sessions sold: July–December 1995

Jul	Aug	Sep	Oct	Nov	Dec
159	203	247	276	235	240

Ensure that the two title lines shown above appear on the chart.

On the vertical axis, put the axis label '**Sessions**'.

On the horizontal axis, put the axis label '**Month**'.

3 Save the chart to your own disk or your own user area under the file name TTNSCHT1.

4 Preview the printout of the chart. Check that the appearance is satisfactory, and that the position on the paper will be suitable, then print the chart.

5 The figures for January 1996 and February 1996 are now available and need to be added to the chart. Add these figures and change the second line of the title to "Table tennis sessions sold: July 1995–February 1996". Make these changes to the chart and save again under the same file name (overwriting the previous version). Make a back-up copy of the file under a different file name.

6 Ensure that the values you entered are displayed on the chart. Print the final version of the chart. In your own handwriting, neatly label the values entered on the printout.

7 List on screen, and then print on paper, the files in the current directory, including the file names for this activity.

8 Exit the chart drawing program.

9 You must now include your chart in a memorandum. Use a word processor program to prepare the heading and introduction for this memorandum. The introduction should describe the information which the chart shows.

10 Use cut and paste (or a similar technique, depending on the software you are using), to transfer the chart to the memorandum. You may need to make adjustments to the layout in order to fit the chart on the page. Add your own short commentary, describing briefly the main features of the information shown in the chart.

11 Save the memorandum, preview and then obtain a printout.

12 Exit the word processor program.

Activity 10.4

SITUATION

You have been given the task of analysing and presenting some statistical information on the use of various sporting activities at Sportstown Leisure Centre. The Centre Manager has told you that it is important that the tables and charts you produce are clear, attractive and well labelled.

CONTENTS

Enter data to specific chart type; add labels; save to disk and print; include chart in memorandum.

Level: INTERMEDIATE
Elements: PREPARE, PRESENT INFORMATION

TASKS

1 Run the chart drawing program.

2 Enter the following data into the program to produce a simple pie bar chart:

Sportstown Leisure Centre

Sources of direct income (£000s): Quarter 1, 1995

Fitness centre	37.1
Squash courts	32.3
Main hall	25.9
Subscriptions	12.3
Clubs	4.7
Parties	2.5
Running track	6.9
Cafe	5.0

Ensure that the two title lines shown above appear on the chart.

Display the money value of each sector of the pie chart.

3 Save the chart to your own disk or your own user area under the file name INCCHT1.

4 Preview the printout of the chart. Check that the appearance is satisfactory, and that the position on the paper will be suitable, then print the chart.

5 Change the chart so that 'Subscriptions' and 'Clubs' are grouped together into one amount called 'Membership'.

6 Make a second change so that, instead of the money value of each sector, the percentage of the total income is shown for each sector. Save the chart again under the same file name (overwriting the previous version). Make a back-up copy of the file under a different file name.

7 Print the final version of the chart. In your own handwriting, neatly label the percentages shown on the printout.

8 List on screen, and then print on paper, the files in the current directory, including the file names for this activity.

9 Exit the chart drawing program.

10 You must now include your chart in a memorandum. Use a word processor program to prepare the heading and introduction for this memorandum. The introduction should describe the information which the chart shows.

11 Use cut and paste (or a similar technique, depending on the software you are using), to transfer the chart to the memorandum. You may need to make adjustments to the layout in order to fit the chart on the page. Add your own short commentary, describing briefly the main features of the information shown in the chart.

12 Save the memorandum, preview and then obtain a printout.

13 Exit the word processor program.

Activity 10.5

SITUATION

You have been given the task of analysing and presenting some statistical information on the use of various sporting activities at Sportstown Leisure Centre. The Centre Manager has told you that it is important that the tables and charts you produce are clear, attractive and well labelled.

CONTENTS

Enter data to specific chart type; add labels; save to disk and print; include chart in memorandum.

Levels: INTERMEDIATE, ADVANCED
Elements: PREPARE, PRESENT INFORMATION

TASKS

1 Run the chart drawing program.

2 Enter the following data into the program to produce a multiple bar chart:

Sportstown Leisure Centre

Visitors to centre: w/b Mon 25 Sep 1995

	Mon	Tue	Wed	Thu	Fri	Sat	Sun
9am–12 noon	143	156	158	204	239	260	328
12 noon–6pm	172	198	190	209	256	237	98
6pm–11pm	207	233	278	281	220	105	79

Ensure that the two title lines shown above appear on the chart.

3 Save the chart to your own disk or your own user area under the file name VISITORS1.

4 Preview the printout of the chart. Check that the appearance is satisfactory, and that the position on the paper will be suitable, then print the chart.

5 Change the chart so that 'Saturday' and 'Sunday' are grouped together into one amount for the week-end.

6 Save the chart again under the same file name (overwriting the previous version). Make a back-up copy of the file under a different file name.

7 Print the final version of the chart. In your own handwriting, neatly label the percentages shown on the printout.

8 List on screen, and then print on paper, the files in the current directory, including the file names for this activity.

9 Exit the chart drawing program.

10 You must now include your chart in a memorandum. Use a word processor program to prepare the heading and introduction for this memorandum. The introduction should describe the information which the chart shows.

11 Use cut and paste (or a similar technique, depending on the software you are using), to transfer the chart to the memorandum. You may need to make adjustments to the layout in order to fit the chart on the page. Add your own short commentary, describing briefly the main features of the information shown in the chart.

12 Save the memorandum, preview and then obtain a printout.

13 Exit the word processor program.

Activity 10.6

SITUATION

You are required to present some sales figures for Wessex Windows, first, in table form, and secondly, in the form of a chart.

CONTENTS

Enter data to specific chart type; add labels; save to disk and print to fit paper of different orientations; include chart in memorandum.

Level: INTERMEDIATE, ADVANCED
Elements: PREPARE, PROCESS, PRESENT INFORMATION

TASKS

1 Run the program on your system which can be used for producing tables.

2 Enter the following figures to the program so that a table is produced, including row and column totals. Label the row and column totals with the word '**Total**'.

Wessex Windows

Regional Sales (£000s): 1995, 4th quarter

Region	October	November	December
South	27.9	26.0	20.9
South-west	18.7	21.9	19.5
South-east	22.0	23.0	20.7
Midlands	11.9	12.7	9.2

The row and column totals should be calculated by yourself if you are using a program which will not do the calculations for you.

3 Save the file to your own disk or your own user area under the file name TABLE1.

4 Preview the printout, make any adjustments necessary so that the table fits on a single sheet of A4 paper (portrait or landscape) and print the table.

5 Select all the text in the table and change it to a different font. Print this second version of the table.

6 Insert an extra region, London, which now needs to be included in the table. The figures for London were as follows:

Region	October	November	December
London	36.1	33.2	24.8

Make any changes which are needed to include the new information in the row and column totals.

7 Select the heading 'Wessex Windows' and make the font for this heading larger than it was, and print the table once more.

8 Save the new version of the table to your own disk or your own user area under the file name TABLE2.

9 Run the chart drawing program. (If necessary on your system, you may need to exit the program you were using for drawing the table.)

10 Using the same figures given above (including those for London), draw a multiple bar chart. This should show bars for the five regions' sales for October grouped together, then the five regions' sales for November grouped together, then the five regions' sales for December grouped together.

11 Preview the chart, make any changes necessary, then print the chart.

12 Save the chart to your own disk or your own user area under the file name REGSALES. Make a back-up copy of the file under a different file name and on a different drive or directory.

13 Change the chart type to a stacked (or component) bar chart, so that the bars for the five regions appear on top of one another. Check the appearance of the chart, then print it. In your own handwriting, neatly label the values for each region, for each month. Choose the most effective of the charts you have printed, and explain on the printout why it is most effective.

14 List on screen, and then print on paper, the files in the directories you have used, including the file names for this activity.

15 Exit the chart drawing program.

16 You must now include your chart in a memorandum. Use a word processor program to prepare the heading and introduction for this memorandum. The introduction should describe the information which the chart shows.

17 Use cut and paste (or a similar technique, depending on the software you are using), to transfer the chart to the memorandum. You may need to make adjustments to the layout in order to fit the chart on the page. Add your own short commentary, describing briefly the main features of the information shown in the chart.

18 Save the memorandum, preview and then obtain a printout.

19 Exit the word processor program.

Activity 10.7

SITUATION

You are required to present some sales figures for Wessex Windows, first, in table form, and secondly, in the form of a chart.

CONTENTS

Enter data to specific chart type; add labels; save to disk and print to fit paper of different orientations; include chart in memorandum.

Level: ADVANCED
Elements: PREPARE, PROCESS, PRESENT INFORMATION

TASKS

1 Run the chart drawing program.

2 Enter the following figures to the program so that a table is produced, including row and column totals. Label the row and column totals with the word 'Total'.

Wessex Windows

National sales (£m):

Product	1992	1993	1994	1995
UPVC windows	9.73	8.45	7.81	9.50
UPVC doors	1.76	1.70	1.12	2.05
Hardwood windows	4.39	4.12	4.08	4.49
Hardwood doors	0.75	0.70	0.42	0.65
UPVC conservatories	8.63	8.73	9.15	9.49
Hardwood conservatories	2.10	2.30	2.58	2.93

The row and column totals should be calculated by yourself if you are using a program which will not do the calculations for you.

3 Save the file to your own disk or your own user area under the file name TABLE3.

4 Preview the printout, make any adjustments necessary so that the table fits on a single sheet of A4 paper (portrait or landscape) and print the table.

5 Select all the text in the table and change it to a different font. Print this second version of the table.

6 Insert an extra column to the right of 1995 and put into this column the estimated sales figures for 1996, which have just been announced by the statistical department at head office. The estimated figures are shown below:

Product	1996
UPVC windows	10.25
UPVC doors	2.50
Hardwood windows	4.70
Hardwood doors	1.00
UPVC conservatories	12.00
Hardwood conservatories	3.50

Make any changes which are needed to include the new information in the row and column totals.

7 Select the heading 'Wessex Windows' and make the font for this heading larger than it was, and print the table once more.

8 Save the new version of the table to your own disk or your own user area under the file name TABLE4.

9 Run the chart drawing program. (If necessary on your system, you may need to exit the program you were using for drawing the table.)

10 Using the same figures given above (including the estimated figures for 1996), draw a multiple bar chart. This chart should show bars for the six products' sales for 1992 grouped together, then the six products' sales for 1993 grouped together, and so on.

11 Preview the chart, make any changes necessary, then print the chart.

12 Save the chart to your own disk or your own user area under the file name NATSALES. Make a back-up copy of the file under a different file name.

13 Change the chart type to a stacked percentage (or 100%) bar chart, so that the bars for the six products appear on top of one another and the vertical axis of the chart shows a percentage scale from 0% to 100%. The bars should all be the same height, and this type of chart will enable you to compare the contributions to total sales made by each of the products. Check the appearance of the chart, then print it. In your own handwriting, neatly label the values for each product, for each year.

14 Choose the most effective of the charts you have printed, and explain on the printout why it is most effective.

15 List on screen, and then print on paper, the files in the current directory, including the file names for this activity.

16 Exit the chart drawing program.

17 You must now include your chart in a memorandum. Use a word processor program to prepare the heading and introduction for this memorandum. The introduction should describe the information which the chart shows.

18 Use cut and paste (or a similar technique, depending on the software you are using), to transfer the chart to the memorandum. You may need to make adjustments to the layout in order to fit the chart on the page. Add your own short commentary, describing briefly the main features of the information shown in the chart.

19 Save the memorandum, preview and then obtain a printout.

20 Exit the word processor program.

Activity 10.8

SITUATION

Draw an organisation chart to show the staffing structure at Sportstown Leisure Centre

CONTENTS

Enter data to specific chart type; add labels; save to disk and print to fit paper of different orientations; include chart in memorandum.

Levels: INTERMEDIATE, ADVANCED
Elements: PREPARE, PRESENT INFORMATION

TASKS

1 Run the program on your system which is used to produce organisation charts.

2 The staff structure at Sportstown Leisure Centre is now described:

The Centre Manager is Ian Whicker; he has overall responsibility for the Leisure Centre. The Assistant Centre Manager, Julie Stones reports to Ian Whicker and is the line manager for the rest of the staff. The rest of the staff are grouped into three areas: Operations, Administration and Maintenance.

In the Operations department are:
John Davey	(Duty officer)
Jackie Stage	(Duty officer)
Phillip Lyons	(Duty officer)

In the Administration department are:
William Graves	(Marketing and promotions)
Susan Gillsman	(Finance officer)
Yourself	(Information technology officer)

In the Maintenance department are:
Six part-time cleaners	
Bill Stage	(Electrician)
Graham Coleman	(Track technician/groundsman)

3 The organisation chart is to be produced on A4 paper. If it is possible to do so on your system, set up the program so that the chart will print on the A4 paper in landscape mode rather than portrait mode. Enter the above names and job description (abbreviated if necessary) at the appropriate levels in order to produce an organisation chart for the Leisure Centre. The six cleaners may be entered into one box.

4 Preview the printout of the chart on the screen. Note that the lowest level may be shown vertically rather than horizontally if necessary in order to fit the chart onto the paper you are using. Print the chart.

5 Save the chart to your own disk or your own user area under the file name ORGCHT1.

6 Ian Whicker is considering appointing an extra staff member in the Administration department to act as a computer network technician.

Put this extra staff member in under the name 'A. N. Other', with the job description 'Network technician'.

7 Save the chart under the new file name ORGCHT2, so that the previous version is kept intact.

8 Preview the printout for this chart. Check the appearance and then print it. In your own handwriting, neatly number the different levels shown on the organisation chart.

9 List on screen, and then print on paper, the files in the current directory, including the file names for this activity.

10 Exit the program which draws organisation charts.

11 You must now include your chart in a memorandum. Use a word processor program to prepare the heading and introduction for this memorandum. The introduction should describe the information which the chart shows.

12 Use cut and paste (or a similar technique, depending on the software you are using), to transfer the chart to the memorandum. You may need to make adjustments to the layout in order to fit the chart on the page. Add your own short commentary, describing briefly the main features of the information shown in the chart.

13 Save the memorandum, preview and then obtain a printout.

14 Exit the word processor program.

Activity 10.9

SITUATION

Draw an organisation chart to show the staffing structure at Wessex Windows.

CONTENTS

Enter data to specific chart type; add labels; save to disk and print to fit paper of different orientations; include chart in memorandum.

Levels: INTERMEDIATE, ADVANCED
Elements: PREPARE, PRESENT INFORMATION

TASKS

1 Run the program on your system which is used to produce organisation charts.

2 The staff structure at the Clearbridge branch of Wessex Windows is now described:

The Branch Manager is David Mullery; he has overall responsibility for the branch. James Kelly reports to David Mullery as Sales manager and is the head of section for the sales team.

The rest of the staff are grouped into two sections: Finance and Secretarial.

In the Finance section are:
John Stebbing
Pam Browne
Clive Horne

In the Secretarial section are:
Doris Knight
Vanessa Green

3 The organisation chart is to be produced on A4 paper. If it is possible to do so on your system, set up the program so that the chart will print on the A4 paper in landscape mode rather than portrait mode. Enter the above names and job description (abbreviated if necessary) at the appropriate levels in order to produce an organisation chart for the Wessex Windows branch office.

4 Preview the printout of the chart on the screen. Note that the lowest level may be shown vertically rather than horizontally if necessary in order to fit the chart onto the paper you are using. Print the chart.

5 Save the chart to your own disk or your own user area under the file name ORGCHT3.

6 David Mullery has just been informed that Vanessa Green has given notice that she will be taking maternity leave. Please replace her with Sheila Strong, who has been working for Wessex Windows on a part-time basis for some years.

7 Save the chart under the new file name ORGCHT4, so that the previous version is kept intact.

8 Preview the printout for this chart. Check the appearance, make any changes necessary, and then print it. In your own handwriting, neatly number the different levels shown on the organisation chart.

9 List on screen, and then print on paper, the files in the current directory, including the file names for this activity.

10 Exit the program which draws organisation charts.

11 You must now include your chart in a memorandum. Use a word processor program to prepare the heading and introduction for this memorandum. The introduction should describe the information which the chart shows.

12 Use cut and paste (or a similar technique, depending on the software you are using), to transfer the chart to the memorandum. You may need to make adjustments to the layout in order to fit the chart on the page. Add your own short commentary, describing briefly the main features of the information shown in the chart.

13 Save the memorandum, preview and then obtain a printout.

14 Exit the word processor program.

Activity 10.10 Scatter chart

SITUATION

Draw a scatter chart to investigate figures at Wessex Windows.

CONTENTS

Enter data to specific chart type; add labels; save to disk and print to fit paper of different orientations; include chart in memorandum.

Level: ADVANCED
Elements: PREPARE, PROCESS, PRESENT INFORMATION

TASKS

1 Run the program on your system which draws scatter charts.

2 The head office of Wessex Windows is looking at the staffing levels at all the branches of the company, to see whether they employ the right number of staff. The statistical department have been asked to look into the connection between the number of staff employed and the sales. Here are the figures collected so far:

Branch number	Staff employed	Sales 1995 (£m)
A	12	26.4
B	7	15.9
C	6	18.7
D	19	30.1
E	5	9.7
F	7	14.2
G	12	23.9
H	10	24.6

3 Enter the number of staff employed as the X-value and the sales for 1995 in £m as the Y-value.

4 Enter 'Wessex Windows branches' as the main title and 'Staff employed and Sales 1995' as a sub-title.

5 Label the X axis (horizontal) as 'Number of staff employed' and label the Y axis (vertical) as 'Sales 1995 (£m)'.

6 Preview the printout of the chart. Make any changes necessary to produce a satisfactory printout and then print the chart.

7 Save the file to your own disk or your own user area under the file name SCATTER1.

8 Label the points on the scatter chart with the branch letters (A, B, C, etc.)

9 Two relatively new branches can now be included in the exercise:

Branch number	Staff employed	Sales 1992 (£m)
I	4	7.3
J	6	8.4

10 Save the file again under the same file name (overwriting the previous file). Also make a back-up copy of the file under a different file name.

11 Preview, make any changes needed, and print the new version of the scatter chart. In your own handwriting, neatly label the branch numbers against the points plotted on the chart.

12 List on screen, and then print on paper, the files in the current directory, including the file names for this activity.

13 Exit the program which draws scatter charts.

14 You must now include your chart in a memorandum. Use a word processor program to prepare the heading and introduction for this memorandum. The introduction should describe the information which the chart shows.

15 Use cut and paste (or a similar technique, depending on the software you are using), to transfer the chart to the memorandum. You may need to make adjustments to the layout in order to fit the chart on the page. Add your own short commentary, describing briefly the main features of the information shown in the chart.

16 Save the memorandum, preview and then obtain a printout.

17 Exit the word processor program.

Activity 10.11 Scatter chart

SITUATION

Draw a scatter chart to investigate figures at Sportstown Leisure Centre.

CONTENTS

Enter data to specific chart type; add labels; save to disk and print to fit paper of different orientations; include chart in memorandum.

Level: ADVANCED
Elements: PREPARE, PROCESS, PRESENT INFORMATION

TASKS

1 Run the program on your system which draws scatter charts.

2 The Sportstown Leisure Centre's Assistant Centre Manager, Julie Stones, is carrying out an exercise to look into the usage of the centre by members of different age groups. She has collected the following information in a randomly selected sample of 12 members:

Member number	Age of member	Average number of visits per month
1	23	4
2	19	11
3	43	4
4	32	3
5	26	7
6	27	9
7	29	6
8	22	9
9	65	7
10	40	5

3 Enter the age of the member as the X-value and the average number of visits per month as the Y-value.

4 Enter 'Sportstown Leisure Centre' as the main title and 'Age against Visits' as a sub-title.

5 Label the X axis (horizontal) as 'Age' and label the Y axis (vertical) as 'Frequency of visits'.

6 Preview the printout of the chart. Make any changes necessary to produce a satisfactory printout and then print the chart.

7 Save the file to your own disk or your own user area under the file name SCATTER2.

8 Label the points on the scatter chart with the member numbers (1, 2, 3, etc.)

9 Two more members can now be included in the chart:

Member number	Age of member	Average number of visits per month
11	16	8
12	23	18

10 Save the file again under the same file name (overwriting the previous). Also make a back-up copy of the file under a different file name and on a different drive or directory.

11 Preview, make any changes needed, and print the new version of the scatter chart. In your own handwriting, neatly label the branch numbers against the points plotted on the chart.

12 List on screen, and then print on paper, the files in the directories you have used, including the file names for this activity.

13 Exit the program which draws scatter charts.

14 You must now include your chart in a memorandum. Use a word processor program to prepare the heading and introduction for this memorandum. The introduction should describe the information which the chart shows.

15 Use cut and paste (or a similar technique, depending on the software you are using), to transfer the chart to the memorandum. You may need to make adjustments to the layout in order to fit the chart on the page. Add your own short commentary, describing briefly the main features of the information shown in the chart.

16 Save the memorandum, preview and then obtain a printout.

17 Exit the word processor program.

11 Presentations

Background to presentations

Visual presentations may be produced with the help of a computer. A presentation in this context is a combination of different types of information, which may include text, charts and diagrams. The presentation is a means of giving information to an audience, whether this is an audience of two people or two hundred people, the aims are the same: to get over the information in as clear and interesting a way as possible.

At Sportstown Leisure Centre, a presentation was recently given to a group of representatives from the national committee of a large sporting organisation. The sporting organisation's committee were looking for a venue in which to hold their South of England championships, and so they read the introductory publicity material for Sportstown Leisure Centre. Following this, a visit to Sportstown Leisure Centre was arranged, in order to find out more, and to compare Sportstown's facilities with those at other venues.

The presentation was designed to show the facilities available at Sportstown Leisure centre, and so William Graves, the Public Relations and Marketing officer for the centre prepared a 30-minute talk. In addition to the notes he used to help him give his talk, William used Presentation software on a PC to prepare a number of slides consisting of text charts, diagrams and pictures to add to the effectiveness of his talk. The PC was linked to a display tablet and an overhead projector, so that the information on the screen of the PC could be seen by all the committee members on a large overhead projector display screen.

At the Clearbridge branch of Wessex Windows, customers who visit the showroom are sometimes given a presentation of the service offered by the company. Again, this presentation is a mixture of text, charts, diagrams and photographs, and has the aim of selling the windows design and fitting service to the customer.

Additionally, David Mullery, the branch manager, makes a twice-yearly report on the progress at the branch over the previous six months to senior managers of the company at head office. Here, a number of charts are used to show the numerical information about sales, customers and costs to best advantage.

Software for presentations

➤➤ **FIND OUT**

Find out what presentation software you are to use. Find out also how to run the presentation program on your system.

The basic features of a presentation program are now described in terms of the types of slides which may be used to make up a complete presentation.

■ Text slides

A text slide comprises several short statements or points. The points are usually separated by a blank line, and may start with an asterisk or bullet. It is important when producing text slides to limit the amount of information on one slide to a few points that can be easily and quickly taken in by the audience. If there is too much material to read through, then the audience will tend only to be distracted from what the presenter of the talk is saying. A rule of thumb is to include five separate points at most, each point consisting of no more than ten words.

■ Chart slides

Chart slides can be any of the following:

- table;
- line chart;
- bar chart;
- pie chart;
- scatter chart;
- high/low/close chart;
- organisation chart.

It is preferable that the chart should not be too complex; the point of including the chart in the presentation is to allow the audience to take in a limited amount of numerical information.

■ Diagram slides

Diagrams such as the floor plans of a the Leisure Centre, or a flow diagram showing the stages involved in ordering, manufacturing, fitting and paying for UPVC window replacements can be displayed as part of a presentation.

■ **Photograph slides**

Some presentation software will enable the user to obtain digitised photographs which are stored in files on disk in the same way as other charts and diagrams, to be included in the range of information in a presentation.

■ **Slide shows**

As well as creating and storing on disk a variety of slides, you can create a slide show by linking a number of slides together. The software will let the user choose the slides to be included in the slide show by highlighting from a list of slides. It will be possible to change the order of the slides in a slide show by using a simple editing feature.

■ **Slide show effects**

You can add effects to a slide show. For example, you can specify how long each slide stays on the screen before the next one is shown, or you may want to move on to the next slide on the press of a particular key.

To add a little interest to the slide show you can tell the program how you want each slide to appear on, and then disappear from, the screen. For example, a slide can be made to scroll up from the bottom of the screen or to fade out from view.

Hardware for presentations

A standard PC system is required for presentation software, with no special requirements for processor or disk drive except in that, as usual with any graphics-based program, the faster the processor and disk drive, the more efficient will be the program to use.

Consideration must be given to how presentations are to be shown to the audience. A large monitor can be used to make the display from the PC visible for the whole audience; these tend to be expensive. Alternatively, as mentioned previously, a display tablet which links up the PC to an overhead projector screen tends to be a much cheaper alternative.

■ Multi-media

Presentation software really comes into its own when it is linked to a variety of multi-media devices. A special camera can be used to store digitised photographs which may become part of a presentation. A scanner is useful for storing paper images and even text in a form which can readily be entered to slides for a presentation. As another example, music and sound effects can be added to a presentation with the hardware devices which are on the market for PCs. There is really a wide range of technology which can be of use here.

➤➤ FIND OUT

> Find out what equipment is available to you to help make a presentation. For example, an overhead projector with a display tablet may be used to display the monitor image onto a large projector screen. Alternatively, it may be possible to link your computer to a large monitor, suitable for an audience.

Activity 11.1 Wessex Windows promotion

SITUATION

Create a text chart for a presentation at Wessex Windows.

CONTENTS

Create chart and enter given text; save to disk and print if possible; vary font sizes to achieve desired effect.

Levels: INTERMEDIATE, ADVANCED

Elements: PREPARE, PRESENT INFORMATION

TASKS

1 Run the presentation program which is available on your system. If you do not have access to specific presentation software, you may use a word processor or a desktop publisher program to produce the text charts for this activity.

2 Create a text chart (or slide) from the following information:

Wessex Windows

- High-quality windows and doors
- Expert fitting service
- Realistic prices and terms of payment
- Established for over 15 years

3 Display the text chart on the screen with the text left-aligned.

4 Select the title of the text chart and centre it.

5 Select the main body of the text in the text chart and centre it.

6 Change the title of the text chart to a larger font size.

7 Save the text chart to your own disk or your own user area under the file name SLIDE.

8 Change the line which says 'Expert fitting service' to 'Precision surveying and fitting'.

9 Save the new version of the chart under the same file name (overwriting the previous file). Also make a back-up copy of the file under a different file name.

10 Print the final version of the text. In your own handwriting, neatly label any lines which are centred, left-aligned or right-aligned.

11 List on screen, and then print on paper, the files in the current directory, including the file names for this activity.

12 Exit the presentation program.

Activity 11.2 Leisure centre facilities presentation

SITUATION

Create and edit text charts for presentations at Sportstown Leisure Centre.

CONTENTS

Create and edit charts and enter given text; save to disk and print if possible; vary font sizes to achieve desired effect.

Levels: INTERMEDIATE, ADVANCED

Elements: PREPARE, PRESENT INFORMATION

TASKS

1 Run the presentation program which is available on your system. If you do not have access to specific presentation software, you may use a word processor or a desktop publisher program to produce the text charts for this activity.

2 The following shows text which has been prepared by William Graves, the Marketing officer at Sportstown Leisure Centre:

Slide 1:

SPORTSTOWN LEISURE CENTRE

- OPENED 1 AUGUST 1989
- BUILT BY SPORTSTOWN DISTRICT COUNCIL
- MANAGED BY HERON MANAGEMENT PLC

Slide 2:

FACILITIES

- FULL-SIZED MAIN SPORTS HALL
- 6 PERSPEX-BACKED SQUASH COURTS
- WELL-EQUIPPED, HIGH-TECH FITNESS CENTRE
- ALL-WEATHER RUNNING TRACK + FIELD SPORTS

Slide 3:

MEMBERSHIP

- EITHER ONE ANNUAL PAYMENT
- OR A MONTHLY SUBSCRIPTION (DIRECT DEBIT)
- FREE TELEPHONE BOOKING CARD
- CHEAPER BOOKINGS

Create three slides for this information. The text should be left-aligned on the screen at this stage. Save them to your own disk or your own user area under the file names SLIDE1, SLIDE2 and SLIDE3.

3 Preview the printout, make any changes necessary and then print a copy of the three slides. Show your lecturer/tutor the slides on the screen so that they can be checked for correct display.

4 Centre the heading and the rest of the text for each of the three slides.

5 Insert an extra point before '• **MANAGED BY HERON MANAGEMENT PLC**'. The new point is '• **SPONSORED BY WESSEX WINDOWS**'.

6 On the third slide, change '**CHEAPER BOOKINGS**' to '**REDUCED PRICES WITH BOOKING CARD**'.

7 Save the new versions under the same file names (overwriting the previous files). Also make back-up copies of the files.

8 Print the final versions of the slides. In your own handwriting, neatly label any lines which are centred, left-aligned or right-aligned.

9 Show the slides on the screen to your lecturer/tutor for checking.

10 List on screen, and then print on paper, the files in the current directory, including the file names for this activity.

11 Exit the presentation software.

Activity 11.3 Wessex Windows promotion

SITUATION

Create and edit text charts for a presentation at Wessex Windows.

CONTENTS

Create chart and enter given text; save to disk and print if possible; vary font sizes to achieve desired effect.

Level: ADVANCED

Elements: PREPARE, PRESENT INFORMATION

TASKS

1 Run the presentation program which is available on your system. If you do not have access to specific presentation software, you may use a word processor or a desktop publisher program to produce the text charts for this activity.

2 The following shows text which has been prepared by James Kelly at Wessex Windows:

Slide 1:

UPVC WINDOWS & DOORS

- LATEST SWEDISH TECHNOLOGY
- DRAUGHT-FREE DESIGN
- SOUND INSULATING VERSIONS AVAILABLE

Slide 2:

HARDWOOD WINDOWS & DOORS

- VERY LONG LASTING
- MADE BY OUR CRAFTSMEN
- SINGLE OR DOUBLE GLAZING

Slide 3:

CONSERVATORY DESIGN SERVICE

- HARDWOOD OR UPVC
- CHOOSE FROM OUR RANGE OF STANDARD SIZES
- OR LET US DESIGN TO SUIT YOUR PROPERTY

Create three slides for this information. The text should be left-aligned on the screen at this stage. Save them to your own disk or your own user area under the file names SLIDE4, SLIDE5 and SLIDE6.

3 Preview the printout, make any changes necessary and then print a copy of the three slides. Show your lecturer/tutor the slides on the screen so that they can be checked for correct display.

4 Centre the heading and the rest of the text for each of the three slides.

5 Insert an extra point before '**MADE BY OUR CRAFTSMEN**'. The new point is '**ATTRACTIVE APPEARANCE**'.

6 On the third slide, change '**HARDWOOD OR UPVC**' to '**HIGH QUALITY MATERIALS**'.

7 Save the new versions under the same file names (overwriting the previous files). Also make back-up copies of the files.

8 Print the final versions of the slides. In your own handwriting, neatly label any lines which are centred, left-aligned or right-aligned.

9 Show the slides on the screen to your lecturer/tutor for checking.

10 List on screen, and then print on paper, the files in the current directory, including the file names for this activity.

11 Exit the presentation software.

12 People and computers

Health and safety issues

It is a legal requirement that computer installations should be designed in such a way that the users of those systems do not suffer health problems, undue stress or discomfort as a result of working for extended periods of time on the computer. The manager and the user must be aware of the requirements for health and safety issues in relation to computer systems.

One reason that there have been problems in the past with computer systems causing discomfort and other ill effects to their users is that, in many instances, these computer systems have introduced substantial changes in the way people work, and these changes have taken place over a relatively short period of time. An example of this is the situation where a secretarial or clerical worker in an office is told that his or her job is to be computerised. Computers, keyboards, monitors and printers and other equipment are bought and delivered. They are unpacked and put into what may seem the best positions in the existing office, with the existing furniture. If this is done, the worker is very unlikely to end up with a system which is comfortable to work with. Many factors have to be considered, such as the height of the desk, the design of the chair to be used and the position of the screen in relation to the windows or other sources of light in the office.

A much better approach is for the office manager, or whoever is responsible for the purchase of equipment and layout of the office, to be aware of the requirements and to design the work station around these requirements, in conjunction with the office worker him-/herself. Some of the health and welfare factors which are important in relation to computer systems are now discussed.

Office furniture

The desk and chair are important elements of the computerised work station. An old desk which was not designed for a computer or other equipment is not likely to be suitable. The desk should have a work space for pen and paper as well as room for the actual computer and other equipment. The keyboard on the work surface should be approximately 0.7 metres (maximum) above the floor if it is to accommodate people of various heights. Sufficient clearance is needed between the knee and the underneath of the desk.

In the same way, the height of the chair should be adjustable, the seat being approximately 0.4 metres above the floor. A stable base for the chair, with castors, is preferable. It is often the case that the worker has to make movements from one end of the desk to the other, perhaps to feed paper into a printer, and the castors make these movements less of a problem. The chair back should also be adjustable to give a comfortable position and lumbar support; back problems have been common for people working all day on computers. Arm rests are not a good idea, as they tend to encourage a poor sitting position.

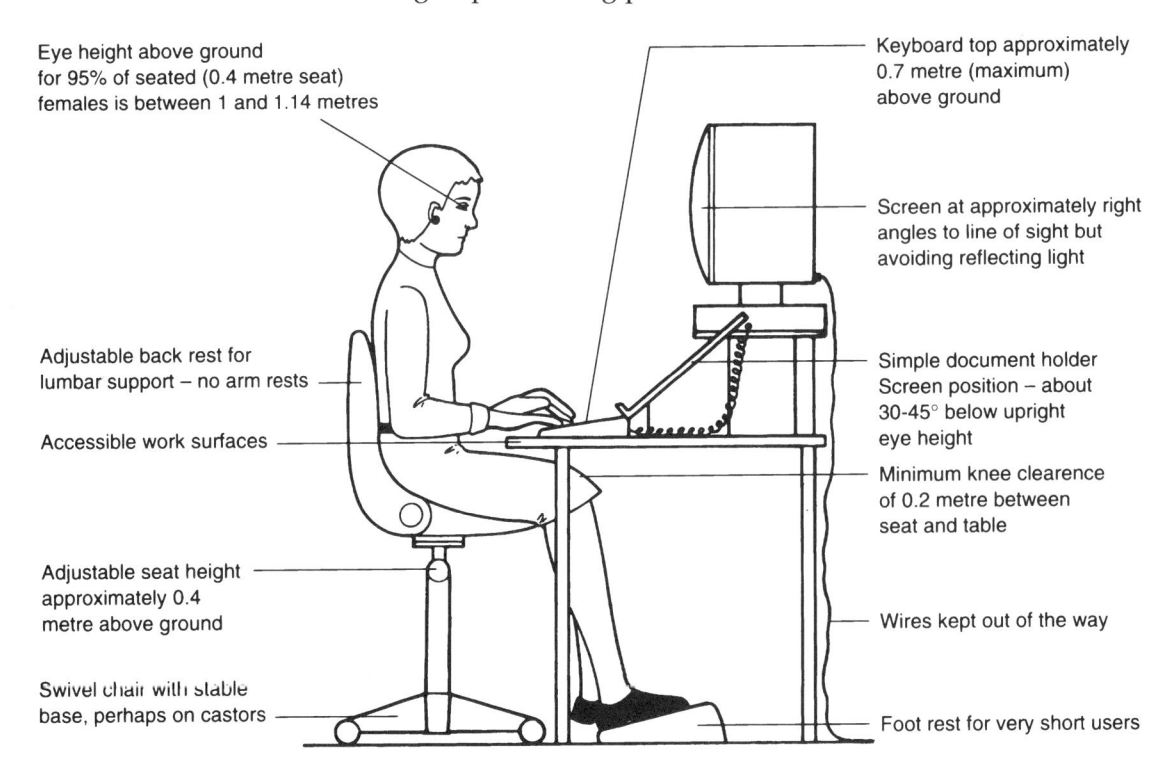

Fig. 17 Office computer system specifications

■ **Monitor**

The screen or monitor should be of the right sort. It should be flicker-free, and should produce an image which is sharp and clear. This requires a good quality monitor, but it also means that the position of the monitor in the room is important, since glare from outside or from lights can make the image difficult to see. A monitor which swivels to alternative positions is preferable to one which is fixed. The height affects the ease of use as well; the screen should be about 30 to 45 degrees below the upright eye height.

■ **Office environment**

The temperature and atmosphere in the office must be suitable for both people and computer equipment. Noise from computer equipment can be extremely irritating. In the past the main culprit here has been the dot matrix impact printer. While these types of printers are being superseded by quieter machines such as ink-jet and laser printers, there are still plenty of older printers in offices, and out-moded ones are still being bought due to their relatively low prices. In a situation where there are going to be more than one or two printers, it is essential that the noise problem is dealt with. If, in the worst case, there are noisy printers, then acoustic hoods are available, which cut out some, but not all, of the noise.

Even the fan inside the CPU box of the ordinary PC can be irritating, and a device can be fitted to cut out the operation of the fan when it is not needed, or to reduce the noise from it.

■ **Leads and sockets**

Unfortunately, every piece of equipment needs its own mains lead. If the office is not properly designed and equipped with mains trunking and sockets at various positions around the room, then one tends to find a mess of leads in the vicinity of every work station. This is both dangerous and displeasing to the eye. Again, it is not expensive to provide enough facilities for the equipment so that the problem does not arise. Trailing leads on the floor should be avoided – they can be tripped over.

■ **Computer software**

As well as the equipment used in computer systems, the software also makes a difference to the comfort or discomfort experienced by the users. Computer software should be designed with the user in mind as well as the actual task to be performed. Ease of use and facilities for obtaining help add to the quality of a program and users should be consulted on the choice of software for a particular task.

■ **Computers users' forum**

One possible answer to these design and layout problems is for the managers who take decisions on equipment and layout to be aware of the requirements, and to be clear that some of these are legal requirements.

A second solution which should also be adopted, and which does exist in many larger organisations, is the computer users' group. This is a body of representatives of both computer users and managers. They meet regularly to discuss problems and find solutions to them in relation to computer systems. Issues of health and safety can be discussed, as well as more general issues, and this type of forum should ensure that the users are provided with systems which are comfortable to work with.

Data security

Data which is kept on computer files instead of in paper filing systems must be kept secure from the danger of loss or corruption. In addition, much of the data which is stored in computer system is personal or business data. This sort of data is private, and it should only be accessed by the appropriate people. Computer systems must be set up and used in such a way as to protect the data that is held in those systems. Indeed, paper filing systems are kept as secure as they need to be, but computer filing systems are much more open to the dangers of loss, corruption and misuse.

Some of the dangers which exist in computer systems are as follows:

- Data may be lost due to equipment failure such as the failure of a disk drive to correctly store or read data on a disk.
- Data may be lost due to a power failure or a sudden variation in the current on a mains power supply (mains 'spikes').

- A fire on the premises can be even more disastrous if important data is lost along with the other damage that the fire causes.
- Errors in computer software known as bugs are surprisingly common, and can cause the loss of data or incorrect processing results. This occurs especially with new software which may not have been sufficiently tested to ensure that it works correctly in all situations.
- Data can be lost or corrupted due to human error, such as the incorrect entry of data, or accidentally issuing commands in a computer system to overwrite files.
- Virus programs are a problem for most computer systems. A virus program is one that has been maliciously written with the intention of causing data loss, either temporary or permanent, in a computer system. The virus will attempt to spread to other computers through communications links or disk transfers. The solution is to install special software which checks for and removes known virus programs from the computer.

■ Backup procedures

The rule when valuable data is stored on a computer system is to make backup copies on secondary disks. Depending on the importance of the data, and the size of the problem that would result if the data were lost, there may be a need to keep two or even three backup copies of files. These should be kept in a secure place in a different location from the original data. For example, if there is a fire, the chances are that all the data in the room or building would be lost. It may be necessary to store backup copies in another building.

The backup copies should be taken regularly. This is not a matter of relying on the whim of users to make backups when they happen to have time or happen to remember. With important data, there should be an agreed procedure which specifies when and how the backups are taken, and whose responsibility it is to make sure that the job is done. For work on PCs, backup copies should be taken at the end of every session (whenever the data on the file has changed) and should be stored in a safe place away from the computer itself.

Larger computer systems usually provide automatic backups at regular intervals. Indeed, this is becoming a feature of even fairly small local area networks; it is programmed into the system software that backup copies are regularly produced.

Fig. 18 3½" floppy disk

■ Floppy disk safeguards

Floppy disks are generally available for personal computers in two sizes: 3.5 inch plastic cased disks and 5.25 inch cardboard cased disks. Both types work in the same way, and they must be treated with care if the user is to keep his or her data safe on them. It is worth spending some time ensuring that data held on floppy disks is safe, as this data may be the result of many hours work. For a business organisation, loss of data on a disk could be a disaster, with the potential loss not only of time and money which has been invested in the past, but also the loss of future business.

The basic rules for floppy disks are as follows:

- Always keep at least one backup copy of important data.
- Make the backup copies regularly, not just when you happen to remember. Have a routine for backing up your disks.
- Do not switch a computer on or off while there is a floppy disk in the drive. This can cause the corruption of files on the disk, making at best a file unreadable, and at worst the whole disk unreadable. Get into the habit of removing your disk from the drive before you switch off.

- Do not remove your disk from the disk drive until you have exited the program you are using. Although you may have saved your file on the floppy disk, most software does not automatically physically write all the data to disk until the file has been properly closed and the program has been exited. This is because the computer writes data to disk in regular-sized blocks; if there is not enough to fill a complete block of data, some data may be held temporarily in a memory buffer area. It is this data which can be lost if you remove the disk before the program is ready, and loss of even a small amount of data in this way can make the file unreadable.
- Do not keep your disks in a bag or pocket where they may get bent.
- Do not touch the exposed surface of the disk with your fingers.
- Do not buy or use poor quality floppy disks. It may be tempting to re-use old disks, or buy new disks at a discount price, but these disks may not be satisfactory. The full price of a disk is insignificant compared to the loss of important information on the disk if it becomes corrupted.
- Ensure that you save to your floppy disk or your network user area at regular intervals while you are working on the computer. It is recommended that you save every five minutes or so – it only takes a few keystrokes to do a save. Some software can be configured so that it saves every few minutes automatically, without being prompted to do so by the user. Find out if this is possible with the programs you use, and switch this feature on when you use the program.
- Use meaningful file names when saving files to disk. With MS–DOS the file name can include up to 8 characters, plus the 3 character file name extension. Although this is rather restrictive in its rules for file names, it is still possible to name your files so that by looking at your directory list you know what was stored in all the files on the disk. This can save a lot of time looking for a particular file, and can help you not to delete files in error.

To summarise the recommended procedures for data security:

- Establish a formal backup procedure. This should be written into procedure manuals.
- Install a backup power supply for systems which store important data. Uninterruptible power supply units (UPS) are available for small computer systems at relatively low cost. For larger systems, a full-scale

power generation unit is used to switch in when the normal power supply fails.

- Use a dual computer system in another place (to avoid loss of data through fire or other catastrophes) for large and important installations. The normal practice is to install a communications link to the dual computer system, so that all the original data can be automatically transferred there at regular intervals.
- Ensure that users of the system are well trained in the procedures for data security.

Data privacy

Data privacy concerns personal data. Most individuals have information regarding ourselves stored in a number of computer files. Even if this is only our name and address (and in most cases it is more than this), it is classed as personal data, and there is a danger of that data falling into the hands of somebody who has no right to see it and may even misuse it. Many people are concerned that personal data held in computer files can too easily be passed on to other people or organisations, and that the data may be inaccurate, out of date or misleading.

This issue has concerned people for a number of years, and the 1984 Data Protection Act was passed with the intention of doing something about this problem. The aim of the Data Protection Act is to safeguard the rights of data subjects (people who have their personal data stored on computer file) by imposing certain obligations on the data users (the people or organisations who keep the files).

The eight principles of the Data Protection Act are as follows:

1. Data shall be obtained fairly and lawfully.
2. Data shall only be held for specified purposes.
3. Data shall not be used in a manner incompatible with those purposes.
4. Data shall be adequate, relevant and not excessive to those purposes.
5. Personal data shall be accurate and kept up to date.
6. Data shall not be kept longer than necessary.
7. Individuals shall be entitled to have access to their data and, where appropriate, to have it corrected or erased.

8 Appropriate security measures shall be taken against unauthorised access to, or alteration, disclosure or destruction of, personal data.

All files of personal data held on computer (with certain specific exceptions) must be registered with the Data Protection Registrar, who has the task of overseeing the enforcement of the Act.

■ Privacy measures

Measures which can be taken to safeguard against unauthorised access to personal data files include the following:

- Only certain employees have access to computer terminals. This may be limited by writing use of the computer terminals into employees' job descriptions, so that it is clear which people are genuine users of the system. The limitation can also apply to time; employees can use the terminals only at particular times during the week.
- Computer rooms and computer terminals require a key or card key to physically unlock them for use.
- Each genuine user has a user identity (User Id) and password; these are required before access to the computer software and/or files is granted by the system. Strict rules may be applied to keeping passwords secret from other users; some companies make revealing your password to another person an offence resulting in dismissal.
- The User Id identifies that user to the computer system; the password (which should be changed from time to time as well as being kept secret) verifies that the user is a genuine user.

Activity 12.1 Health and safety requirements

SITUATION

Write a memorandum to staff giving advice on health and safety issues.

CONTENTS

Create document of required layout; save to disk; print to fit paper; explain health and safety issues.

People and computers 231

Levels: INTERMEDIATE, ADVANCED

Elements: PREPARE, PRESENT INFORMATION
EVALUATE THE USE OF I.T.

TASKS

1 For this activity, you are to take the role of the chairperson of the Computer Users Group at Sportstown Leisure Centre. You are to produce a memorandum to all staff on the subject of health and safety requirements for computer systems. Run the word processor program on your system.

2 Create a new file, and set up the page so that a memorandum may be produced, with the following layout at the top of the page:

MEMORANDUM

To: Date:

From: Ref:

Following a recent discussion at the IT User Group monthly meeting, it was decided to issue a summary of health and safety requirements for computer systems to all staff at the centre.

Please keep to the following guidelines when working with the computers:

1   Work in a comfortable position by adjusting the screen and the height of the chair at your work station.

Note that the heading '**MEMORANDUM**' should be centred.

3 You are to address the memorandum to 'All staff' at the Sportstown Leisure Centre, and it is from yourself. It is on the subject of health and safety requirements for the computer systems at the centre. Give today's date; the reference is 'IT User Group'.

4 Please add another five points to the memorandum, to cover the main areas of concern with regard to health and safety.

5 Use the spell checker and correct any mistakes.

6 Preview the printout of the memorandum and make any adjustments necessary in order to obtain a satisfactory printout.

7 Save the memorandum to your own disk or your own user area under the file name HEALTH1. Also make a back-up copy of the file under a different file name.

8 Print the final version of the memorandum. In your own handwriting, neatly label the positions in the text where you have used the tab key, and where text has been centred.

9 List on screen, and then print on paper, the files in the current directory, including the file names for this activity.

10 Exit the word processor program.

Activity 12.2 Floppy disk advice

SITUATION

Write a report on the recommended procedures for staff using disks to store important data.

CONTENTS

Create document; save to disk; print to fit paper; explain data security issues.

Levels: INTERMEDIATE, ADVANCED

Elements: PREPARE, PRESENT INFORMATION
           EVALUATE THE USE OF I.T.

TASKS

1 Run the word processor program on your system.

2 Staff at Wessex Windows have experienced some difficulty with storing data files on floppy disks and on the hard disks of some of the laptop personal computers. This has wasted considerable time in some cases, as important work which has been lost has had to be entered into the computers again. In a few instances, staff have completely lost records of orders and work done, meaning a loss of business to the company.

It may be that staff are not using their disks properly, and are not taking proper backup precautions for their files, in which case they need to be reminded of the proper procedures. They have all been on introductory training courses for the use of PCs, but a reminder now may improve the situation.

Please write a short report (approximately 750 words) on recommendations for staff using computers in Wessex Windows on how to keep files safe from the risk of data loss and corruption. Include information and recommendations on the following areas:

- purchasing disks;
- formatting disks;
- virus checks;
- backup procedures;
- physical storage of floppy disks.

3 When you have completed your report, use the spell checker to correct any mistakes of spelling, do a visual check of the document on the screen. Save the file to your own disk or your own user area under the file name SAFETY1.

4 Make a back-up copy of the file under a different file name.

5 Preview and print the final version of the document. In your own handwriting, neatly label the positions in the text where you have used the tab key, and where text has been centred, left-aligned or right-aligned.

6 List on screen, and then print on paper, the files in the current directory, including the file names for this activity.

7 Exit the word processor program.

Activity 12.3

SITUATION

Carry out a survey and make a report on health and safety at your place of work or study.

CONTENTS

Investigate and report on the use of computer equipment, errors, faults and hazards; recommend corrective actions, stating responsibility for such actions.

Levels: INTERMEDIATE, ADVANCED

Elements: PREPARE, PRESENT INFORMATION
EVALUATE THE USE OF I.T.

TASKS

1 Carry out a survey of computer work stations and/or computer rooms at you place of work or study.

2 In your survey, note down any health and safety hazards for computer operators or equipment, relating in particular to:

- seating;
- lighting;
- screen orientation;
- cables/power supplies;
- work surfaces;
- dangers of damage to equipment or corruption to disk storage.

3 Write up a report on your findings, on a word processor. For each item given in (2) above, state:

- whether there is a hazard;
- the nature of the hazard;
- recommended corrective action.

4 Also state whether the user at the work station should correct the fault and, if not, who has responsibility for it.

5 Save your file, apply a spell checker and check your document visually on the screen before printing.

6 Make a back-up copy of the file under a different file name.

7 In your own handwriting, neatly label on the printout the positions in the text where you have used the tab key, and where text has been centred, left-aligned or right-aligned.

8 List on screen, and then print on paper, the files in the current directory, including the file names for this activity.

9 Exit the word processor program.

Activity 12.4

SITUATION

Design and print a poster to Sportstown Leisure Centre informing staff of the recommended procedures for the handling and treatment of floppy disks.

CONTENTS

Choose appropriate layout for DTP page; summarise some data security issues.

Level: ADVANCED

Elements: PRESENT INFORMATION
 EVALUATE THE USE OF I.T.

TASKS

1 Run the desktop publisher program on your system.

2 Design a simple poster with large-sized text, stating four rules for the treatment of floppy disks. The poster will be prominently displayed next to the computer work stations at Sportstown Leisure Centre.

3 Save the document to your own disk or your own user area under the file name POSTER1.

4 Preview the printout of the document, make any adjustments necessary in order to obtain a satisfactory printout, and print the poster.

5 Exit the desktop publisher program.

13 Hardware for information technology

Introduction to information technology (IT)

Information technology (IT) is used in nearly all areas of business, commerce and leisure. By definition, IT is the use of computers and other associated devices for the collection, storage and manipulation of data to produce, present and communicate information.

Advantages and disadvantages of IT

Most people are aware of the importance of computers and information technology in modern society, but you should also be clear as to the advantages and the disadvantages of using computerised systems rather than older, 'pen and paper' systems.

■ Advantages

The advantages of using a computer system for such tasks include the following:

- Computerised processing is much faster than manual processing.
- The information produced by a computerised system will in general be more accurate than that resulting from a manual system.
- Many boring, repetitive and time-consuming tasks can be done by computer, thus freeing staff to carry out other duties.
- The information produced by a computerised system will be more

flexible than with a manual processing system; for example, a set of numbers can be presented on a computer screen in several alternative forms (e.g. as a list, as a table of figures or as a graph).

- Information, once produced by a computerised system is already in a form suitable for communicating to other people or organisations.

■ Disadvantages

Some disadvantages of computerised systems are:

- Increased reliance on technology, which may cause problems if it fails; for example, if the computer breaks down or there is a power cut.
- The need for training of staff to operate a computerised system. This is time consuming and expensive, but unless it is done, staff will not get the most out of the systems they are using.
- Information technology equipment becomes obsolete quite quickly, due to the fast rate at which new developments come onto the market. This means that it is expensive to keep up to date. Of course, particularly in a business situation, it is important to keep up to date with the technology; if you do not do so you may lose customers to competitors in the industry with more up-to-date IT systems, who will be able to offer customers a better, more efficient service.

Data

You should regard information technology as a tool which is needed to carry out a huge variety of tasks. The aim of using IT is the efficient production of information. The starting point of information technology is data. Data can be thought of as raw facts and figures. These facts and figures must be collected and put into a form which the computer system can deal with. The data may be of several different types:

Numeric data

Numeric data can be of different types, for example whole numbers, decimal numbers, percentages or even dates and times. Amounts of money which have been received in payment for goods purchased by a customer may be the data which is input to a computer system.

Textual data

Text – for example the text of a letter which is being typed into a word processor program on a personal computer – is a form of data. This may be entered through a keyboard; alternatively it may be input to a computer from a scanner, a device which reads the text printed on paper.

Graphical data

Graphical data, consists of lines, shapes, coloured areas or even moving lines and shapes. The data will normally be stored by the computer in the form of numbers, but the most common method of producing the lines and shapes is to draw them on a computer screen with the help of a mouse or other 'pointing' device. A diagram which shows the layout of flower bed, lawns and paths in the plan of a garden may be produced on a computer system, and this would consist in part of graphical data.

Mixed data

Much data is a mixture of these types. For example, the plans of a garden given in the previous example, would include graphical data to show the layout of the garden, textual data in the form of labels for the different features , and numeric data to show the dimensions of the various features. All these data types would be stored in the computer for this one application.

■ Storage

The data which is fed into a computer system must then be stored. The storage of the data is done by the hardware of the computer system itself, but the user has to be aware of how and where the storage is done, so as to ensure that the data can be retrieved at a later time, and also to check that the storage has been done successfully.

For personal computers the data may be stored either on floppy disk (3.5 inch or 5.25 inch), or on hard disk. The hard disk is actually permanently fixed inside the main box of the computer, but it stores data in just the same way as the floppy disk. Most PC systems identify the various disk drives which are attached to the computer by a letter, such as A or B which represent the floppy disk drive(s) and C or D which represent the hard disk drives(s). On a network computer system the drives in use for users of the network may have a variety of letters as names, depending upon how the system has been set (configured) by the network manager.

■ Processing

Once the data for a particular job on the computer has been stored, it will generally be processed in some way. The aim of processing the data is to manipulate or rearrange it in some way so that it becomes more useful than the original information. Processing consists of calculations and logical steps which are done under the control of the program, or software, which the computer is running at the time.

Processing Wessex Windows data

An example of processing is when Wessex Windows surveyors take a laptop personal computer to a customer for the purpose of recording the measurements of the window and door openings. Once the measurements have been taken they are entered through the keyboard to the memory (and the disk storage) of the computer. The processing which then takes place consists of a large number of fairly complex calculations, which several years ago had to be done by the surveyor by hand with the help of pen, paper and calculator. Now the laptop PC is preprogrammed with software that will make all the calculations necessary to output the window designs, materials needed and costs of manufacture and fitting. In this way the customer gets a quotation on the price of the job very quickly, and the surveyor can be sure that the results are correct, as long as the original measurements were correctly taken and entered.

Central processing unit

The central processing unit (CPU) has the function of carrying out arithmetical and logical operations, rather like a glorified calculator. The CPU is actually the main circuits of the computer, and for a PC is located in the main box of the PC (sometimes called the CPU box). Although there is a similarity between the CPU and a calculator, the big difference between the two is that the CPU can process a large number of operations and instructions very quickly and automatically. The calculator must be given individual instructions one by one which it then carries out in turn. Some calculators can be programmed, and they then become more similar to a computer.

The speed of operation of the CPU is essential to the work of the computer system as a whole. A single addition of two numbers, for example, may take a computer only a thousandth of a millionth of a second to carry out. This is the basic reason why computers are so useful to us; they can carry out millions upon millions of separate operations in seconds.

The other parts of the CPU are the main memory and the control unit.

■ The main memory

While a computer is in use, there is an area of storage inside the computer called the RAM (random access memory). This RAM is made of electronic components in the form of integrated circuitry, or chips. The RAM of a computer system is temporary storage: that is, when the computer is switched off the contents of the RAM memory will be lost. Because it is only a temporary storage, the user must make sure that any data or information which is to be kept is stored on a more permanent storage device, which will usually be a disk drive.

The RAM stores:

- System software such as the operating system, parts of which must be present in RAM at all times in order for the computer to be usable. When you first switch on a PC the operating system is 'booted up' or loaded into the RAM. This sets up the computer for use by other programs such as a word processor or accounts program.
- The program currently being run.
- The data which the user has fed into the computer for processing or storage.
- The information which is the result of processing.

With today's computer systems the loading of a program into memory typically takes only a few seconds; if you are using a less powerful PC to run recently produced software, it may take up to half a minute to load. Then the computer starts to carry out the instructions in the program. The program continues to run until the user gives a command to exit the program. All the time the program is in use it is occupying the RAM.

Processor types

The processor is the most important component in the PC which determines how powerful the computer is, and therefore how effectively it does its job. Although the processor is only one of the chips on the circuit board inside the CPU box of a PC, it is the central component which decides how the rest of the system works.

Computer technology changes quickly, and there is range of different types of processor chips available to the user at any point in time. The majority of PCs in the world use one of just a few processor types.

The 8086

The 8086 processor was the processor which powered the original IBM Personal Computer when it came onto the market in the early 1980s. This processor can still be used, and many users still work quite happily with computers which rely on this processor. What you will find if you use a PC based around this processor is that the computer will seen to run very slowly compared to the latest computers. There will be a significant delay between giving a command and the computer responding. The length of the delay will depend upon the particular command you have given and the particular software being used, but the delay will still be there. With a modern program, such as Microsoft Windows version 3.1, which makes full use of WYSIWYG screen displays, the software may either be impossible to use with this type of processor or it may run so slowly as to be effectively not worth using.

The 286

The 286 processor runs faster and can be used to run Windows and other software requiring WYSIWYG screen displays, but it may not be fast enough for some software. Again, the delay in reacting to commands may be too long for some applications.

The 386

The 386 processor comes in two varieties: the 386SX and the more powerful 386DX. These processors will run nearly all if not all software which is available today, but they may not be fast enough to cope with particular applications such as computer-aided design or desktop publishing.

The 486

The 486 processor, which also comes in an SX and a DX version is relatively new to the scene and should have no problems with any of today's software.

The Pentium

Finally the most recent processor is called the Pentium, and this forms the basis of much new software for the next few years. Pentium processors vary in speed; from 60MHz to 133MHz.

To summarise, the user ought to be aware of the processor which is inside the machine he or she is using simply from the point of view of knowing what performance to expect from different software programs. The latest technology will be needed to provide a platform for all software for the next few years, but for most users it is not essential to operate with the very latest technology.

Floppy disks

Floppy disks come in two sizes: 3.5 inch disks which are contained inside a hard plastic casing, and 5.25 inch disks in cardboard covers. In recent years the 3.5 inch version has become much more common than the other size.

The 3.5 inch disk is a circular plastic disk coated in a magnetisable material, and data is stored on it in binary magnetic form as magnetic 'spots'. These magnetic 'spots' represent ones and zeros, the basis of the binary number system, and this is, in fact, how all computer data is stored internally. The software in the computer is what converts textual, numeric and graphical data into binary form when it needs to be stored on the surface of the disk, and converts it back to the required format when data is being read from the disk.

The data is placed on concentric rings on the disk's surfaces, known as tracks. Each track is split up into sectors to make units of storage. On the outside tracks of a disk is placed an index of the address or location of each block of data which is stored. All this is done automatically by the hardware and software of the computer, and the user plays no part in this process except to give a file name for data, which is to be stored or retrieved.

Modern 3.5 inch floppy disks must be formatted on the computer before they can be used for data storage. The formatting process again is carried out by the computer software, and it amounts to the computer laying out markers on the surface of the disk for the position of each track and sector. Most disks are double-sided, and they can be formatted to different densities of data.

You should always make sure that the disks you are using for storing files are of good quality, and are formatted to the density recommended by the manufacturer. Recent PCs format disks to 1.44 megabytes (called 'high density') or 720 kilobytes (called 'double density'), but older systems may only be able to cope with 360 kilobytes. It is best to use high density disks, as these may be formatted to any of the densities mentioned.

Hard disk storage

Hard disks operate in a very similar way to floppy disks. The data stored on them is placed in the form of binary magnetic spots. The difference is that, because the hard disk drives are fixed inside the PC and are not exchangeable, they can be made to revolve at faster speed and the read/write heads which store and retrieve data on the disk surface can be made to move with greater precision. This results in faster operation and much higher-capacity disks. The typical minimum capacity of a hard disk drive for a PC today is 200Mb which means that it can store over 150 times as much as a high density floppy disk.

If required, you can obtain disk drives of much larger capacities, and this is necessary in some situations due to the large size of modern computer software. A modern PC program, when installed on the hard disk drive can take up as much as 30 or 50Mb of the disk's capacity. If a system needs several programs as large as this, and extra room for the operating system software and for data files, the 200Mb of a drive can quickly become full.

Optical disc storage

Although floppy disk and hard disk drives work perfectly well, much larger storage capacities are available with optical storage, known as CD–ROM (compact disc read only memory). The data here is stored in a different way, essentially the same as on an audio compact disc. The method of reading from the disc is 'safer', because there is not the danger which exists with magnetic disk storage that the read/write head will make contact with the surface of the disk (called a 'head crash'), destroying the data on the disk.

Fig. 19 CD ROM

At present this technology is read only, that is, the user cannot store his or her own files on the CD–ROM. The capacity of a CD–ROM is more than 650 Mb – the same as nearly 500 floppy disks. Common applications for CD–ROM at present are for the storage of encyclopaedias and other reference information, as well as software collections (such as computer games) and computer based training systems.

Upgrading

Computer systems are upgradable. This means that they can be altered or added to to make them capable of carrying out different jobs, and, in particular, to make them more powerful. The most common reason for upgrading a PC is to improve the speed at which it operates a required software package. In order to upgrade a PC, the following upgrades are available.

■ Add extra RAM

To improve the performance in running a particular program, extra RAM may be added to the computer. The PC was originally designed to have a RAM size of 512 or 648 kilobytes. For current software, this size of RAM would not be enough in most cases, so that the PCs which are on the market come with 4, 8, 16 or more megabytes of RAM. Even so, the user often finds that extra performance is needed, and this upgrade option is relatively cheap and easy to carry out. The RAM comes on small boards, usually called SIMMS. These are fitted into spare sockets on the board inside the PC, and as long as there are enough spare sockets for the memory upgrade which is required, there is no problem for the user in doing this. Sometimes, switches on the computer's board have to be changed or set.

■ Adding a co-processor

A co-processor is an extra processor chip which may be fitted into the PC, and it takes over and speeds up some of the arithmetical operations of the computer. This upgrade is only effective if the software in use has been written to work with a co-processor, and the most common applications are ones which involve a large amount of mathematical calculations, such as a graphic design program. (The computer has to carry out large numbers of calculations continuously in order to store and update the graphical images on the screen.)

■ Changing the processor

Some computers have been designed so that it is possible to change to a different processor chip. The reason for this is to make the computer last longer before it becomes obsolete. It is attractive to individuals and businesses to buy computers which can be modernised at relatively low expense at some time in the future. This 'upgradability' is a relatively new feature of PCs.

■ Adding a new disk drive

In order to increase the storage capacity of the computer, a new or an extra hard disk drive can be added, as long as there is room inside the PC.

■ Adding a graphics card

Various 'cards' may be inserted into sockets inside a PC to improve the performance of the graphic screen display. This has been a common requirement for users who have started to used programs such as Microsoft Windows which make heavy demands on the computer from the point of view of the screen display.

Monitor

The monitor of the computer is a vital part of the system, since if the user cannot obtain a satisfactory display of the information being produced, then the computer system is of little value. The monitor may be monochrome or colour, and colour displays are really needed for most applications. The only exception to this is if the PC is only being used for text-based software. For example a PC used exclusively as a word processor may only need a monochrome monitor. However, software is written

Fig. 20 PC monitor

for colour monitors, and the menus and other screen features may become more difficult to use if colour is not available.

The sharpness, or 'resolution' of the screen display is a vital element. If you are working on a computer for significant lengths of time, you must have a sharp image on the screen. Over the years there have been a number of different 'standards' in monitor resolutions. These standards are a result of a combination of the technology in the monitor itself which produces the colours on the screen, and the circuitry inside the computer which ensures that the right signals are sent to the monitor.

The display standards include:

- Hercules graphics
- CGA
- EGA
- VGA
- Super VGA

Each has a different resolution. To understand what the resolution of a screen means, you need to be clear that the display on any screen is made up from a number of tiny dots of coloured light. These are called pixels (picture elements) and any image on the screen, whether it be text or graphics, is made up from the appropriate combination of pixels. The higher-resolution displays contain more pixels. For example, a VGA display may be 1024 by 768 pixels. This means that the screen shows 750 000 pixels to produce the display.

In addition to the number of pixels, another factor is the number of colours which are available. This can be anything from just two for a monochrome monitor to millions of colours being available on some monitors.

Keyboard

The keyboard attached to the computer is a fairly standard affair. Whether you use a terminal to a mainframe computer, a standard PC or a small laptop personal computer, the layout of the characters on the keyboard will be the standard QWERTY arrangement. (QWERTY are the first six letters on the top letter row of the keyboard.) There are differences, however. Looking at a keyboard, it is clear that there are a lot more than letters available. There are all the punctuation marks, numbers, cursor control keys and other special keys such as the **<Enter>** key and the **<Caps lock>** key. On smaller laptop computers in particular, these keys may not be in the position you have come to expect. Small keyboards have been designed for these laptops, but they have sometimes been developed by changing the positions of some of the special keys.

Most keyboards have function keys; either ten or twelve of them. These are used in different ways according to the program which is in use. The word processing program Word Perfect, for example, makes full use of the function keys to carry out commands. By combining the pressing of the twelve function keys with three other keys – the **<SHIFT>**, **<CTRL>** and **<ALT>** keys, it is possible to set up 39 different commands on the function keys.

Some programs allow the user to set up or configure the function keys. You can specify what you want the function keys to do, and this can save a lot of time on operations, or sequences of operations that are often carried out whilst using that program.

■ Mouse

The mouse is the usual addition to the keyboard as a means of data entry. The role of the mouse can be:

- To move a pointer on the screen as the user moves the mouse around the surface of the desk.
- By clicking a button on the mouse, a choice can be made from an on-screen menu.
- By 'clicking and dragging' the mouse it is possible to draw various shapes and lines on the screen when using a drawing program. In addition, in the drawing program the mouse can be used to select which tool to use, perhaps the paintbrush, the paint roller or an eraser.
- In Microsoft Windows File Manager program, the mouse can be used to move files from one directory area on disk to another by the method of clicking and dragging. Alternatively, by holding down a special key while the mouse is being dragged, the user can copy rather than move a file.

The information given above shows that a mouse is virtually essential to the operation of most modern programs. A keyboard alternative is always provided, however, for users who either do not have a mouse available, or simply prefer to use the keyboard.

Mouse design

The actual design of the mouse – its shape, size and the positions of the buttons – is important if you are using a mouse for a long period of time, because users have found that it can result in strain on the wrist and arm. Other designs are available, other than the traditional one where the mouse has a ball underneath to register movement on the desk. Laptop PCs can be equipped with a smaller roller-ball device which attaches to the edge of the keyboard. This performs the same function as the mouse, but can be used without access to a desktop.

Mainframe computers

A mainframe computer is a large, very powerful computer, used generally by large companies and organisations. It is physically large enough to need a special room to accommodate the central processing unit together with some of its peripheral devices such as magnetic disk drive units, tape drive units, printers and communications equipment.

A mainframe computer can support a large number of different users at the same time. These users will typically all be linked up to the mainframe computer from their own terminals or standard PCs. A terminal (sometimes called a dumb terminal) has no processing power of its own; it is essentially just a keyboard and screen used for input to and output from the central mainframe computer. Some terminals may have disk storage attached to the terminal so that users can store their data on their own floppy disks, for instance; other terminals may have some limited capability to process information without continually accessing the mainframe.

Some mainframes are capable of supporting hundreds or even thousands of users, each at their own terminal, at the same time. Because of the fact that the mainframe is very powerful, it can deal with each user's processing requirements in turn at a very fast rate, and so it should appear to each user that they have sole use of the computer. In other words, there is no delay in response to each user's data entry.

One typical use of a mainframe computer is in a large college or university. Several hundred terminals situated in different buildings on the university campus may be connected to a central mainframe, and the students can work on any application program which is held in the mainframe computer's central storage units.

There is a limit, of course, to the power of the mainframe in this type of situation. The university authorities cannot go on adding to the number of terminals without there being eventually a deterioration in the response time noticed by the users. (The response time is the time taken for the computer to accept input data, do the processing necessary, and reply in the form of output on the user's screen.)

Mainframe computers are not used solely by people in the same building or on the same site. It is quite common for the data on a mainframe computer to be made available to users the whole world over, via international cable and telephone networks. Or it may be that a large company has a mainframe at head office together with hundreds of PCs for its staff throughout the various branches of the organisation. Users may want to use the PC simply in 'stand-alone' mode, without connecting through to the mainframe, or they may want at other times to access central files for the company on the mainframe at head office.

Mid-range computers

A minicomputer, or mid-range computer, is a small version of a mainframe computer and is used for applications where the volume of data to be processed at any time is not large enough to warrant the expense of a large mainframe system. Mid-range computers are quite common in industry as a means of providing processing power to an office or a few offices to carry out some specific business task.

A typical application of a mid-range system is in the accounts department of a small to medium-sized organisation. The CPU is housed in a cabinet in one corner of the room, and there are eight terminals attached to the CPU. These terminals are used by account office staff to enter transactions, make queries and obtain information from the accounts system. The system has been sold to the organisation as a complete solution, and as well as the accounts software, the staff can also use word processor and spreadsheet programs. The system runs under a version of the UNIX operating system, and data is stored on standard-sized floppy disks.

Printing devices

- ## Dot matrix printer

    This is by far the most widely used printer for personal computer systems today, although it is fast being caught up by other types. The printer is designed for the printing of text, although graphics can be produced.

    The dot matrix printer produces the shapes of the printed characters by hammering metal pins against an ink ribbon to produce the image on the paper. These pins are arranged so that, as the print head moves across the paper in a straight line, different combinations of the pins produce the different characters. Due to the fact that the pins are forcibly hammered against the ribbon, the dot matrix printer is extremely noisy. The noise can be cut down to some extent by keeping the area around the print head covered, or it is possible to enclose the entire printer in an acoustic hood, but this is not a complete solution. The quality of output from the dot matrix printer will depend on the capacity of the model used. There are two models available.

    ### *9-pin dot matrix*

    First, the printer may be a 9-pin dot matrix. With 9 pins arranged vertically, the shape of each character is not smooth; it is clear from looking at the printout that the characters are made up from a series of dots. An improvement on this is available with most 9-pin printers, called 'near letter quality' (NLQ). With NLQ, the print head makes two passes across each line, the first usually from left to right, the second from right to left. On the second pass the print head is moved vertically a very small distance, enough to make the second set of dots fill in the gaps between the first set of dots. This results in a noticeable improvement in the quality of the printed characters, but the downside is that it takes time; the speed of operation with NLQ is cut drastically.

    ### *24-pin dot matrix*

    A 24-pin dot matrix printer produces printed characters of much higher quality, and at a greater speed, than with a 9-pin model. There are usually several fonts available which can be set by buttons on the printer itself (in addition to the fonts which can be made available in the software being used). A font is the name given to the precise shape and size of printed characters.

Even with a 24-pin printer, the reader can still tell that the output is produced on a dot matrix device; the characters are made up from a number of dots. Although the output will be perfectly clear to readers, there is a tendency for people to become used to computer output which is as good in quality as the highest currently available, which would be from a laser printer. Businesses in particular may find that they need to send the highest possible output quality to customers. In addition, the 24-pin printer still suffers from the noise problem in common with all types of impact printer.

Colour printers of this type are available, and they work by using ribbons made up from several strips of different colours. This feature can be useful, and adds a lot to the effectiveness of the output when used properly. However, it is important to realise that colour printing will only work from software which has been written to make colour available. For example, if you intend to print word-processed documents which include some coloured words or sentences, there has to be a method of selecting the areas of text and setting it to a certain colour. In addition, the correct printer driver must be used for the make and model of colour printer you are using. (See the section on printer drivers in this chapter.)

■ Ink-jet and bubble-jet printers

A good solution to the problem of noise in dot matrix printers has been provided by the ink-jet and bubble-jet printers. The problem is solved by squirting a tiny dot of ink directly onto the paper; this makes no noise at all. The dot of ink is electrically controlled, and the only significant disadvantage is that the ink may take some time to dry.

The quality of output is high, but not perfect; in other words, the shape of each character is not precisely defined by perfectly straight lines and perfectly smooth curves. These printers are seen as a realistic cheaper alternative to laser printers. Also, there are some excellent smaller versions available which are marketed as portable printers, approximately the size of an A4 notebook personal computer.

As with 24-pin dot matrix printers, colour versions are available. There are several coloured jets located in the print head; in addition, the ink colours may be combined to produce a wide range of different colours.

■ **Thermal printer**

Thermal printers produce their output by applying heated pins to special heat-sensitive paper. It is this which is the biggest disadvantage of the thermal printer; you cannot use normal paper. The printer is virtually silent, however. Currently, the most common application of thermal printing is in special-purpose applications, such as printing from hand-held computers and other devices.

■ **Laser printer**

The laser printer is the perfect answer to most printing requirements. Its only drawback until relatively recently has been its cost, but this is reducing rapidly as the laser becomes the standard business paper output device.

A laser printer produces its copy in an entirely different way from the printers mentioned so far; in fact, in some ways it is closer in design to a photocopier. An image of the required document is built up electrostatically on the drum of the laser printer, and 'toner' – a powder made from very fine particles of black plastic – is transferred from this to the paper when they come into contact. The toner is melted onto the surface of the paper to make it stick. A page is printed at a time rather than a line at a time, as with the other types of printer.

The laser printer has been designed to produce graphics just as easily as it can produce text, and the text characters should be perfectly produced, with straight lines and clear curves to produce the shape of each printed character (as long as the correct printer driver is used). Again because of the basic design of the laser printer, it is easy (as long as the software permits it) to print scalable characters. This means that if you have chosen a particular font, you can decide on a wide range of sizes of characters in that font. You can use scalable fonts to make posters, for example, with some large and some small lettering on the same sheet.

There is a range of different types of laser printer available, and the precise set of features offered will affect its purchase price. The features offered include the following.

Printing speed

The speed of a laser printer is usually measured in terms of the number of pages per minute that it can print. This may be anything from 4 to 20 pages per minute. However, this measure does not really give the user a true indication of the speed at which work can be produced on a laser printer. The number of pages per minute may be correct for data which has already been sent to the printer, but when in use a large amount of time is spent by the computer in sending the right data through to the printer. Sending a file to a laser printer is a far more complex process (for the computer and printer) than sending a simple document from a word processor to a dot matrix printer for instance.

Paper handling facilities

A laser printer may use a single bin for paper, or two bins, which enables the user to change quickly to a different size of paper. Single sheet feeding may also be required from time to time.

Resolution

This is the sharpness or resolution of the printed output.

Memory

The memory available in the laser printer is a very important factor in assessing its effectiveness. Most laser printers can print in two alternative ways. First, the page to be printed can be sent to the laser printer as a bit image. This means that the computer and printer have to store each 'slice' of the printed page as a series of tiny dots. The whole page is eventually built up from millions of these dots. The method works perfectly well, but it can be slow and expensive in use of memory. The bigger memory the laser printer has, the better it is able to deal with these bit image files.

The second method of sending data for the printing of a page is to use a page description language. This is a mathematical programming language, which is capable of defining shapes, lines areas and even textual characters in the commands of the language. The method is more economical and faster then the bit image method, especially for pages which contain a variety of graphical and textual information. A common page description language is called 'postscript'. There are different versions of the postscript language in use, but another advantage of this method of printing is that the postscript file can be printed on any printer which is 'postscript compatible'. The language has become a standard method of page description across a number of different printers.

Memory modules may be added to a laser printer to increase its power, and extra cartridges can be installed, for instance to convert a bit image laser printer to one which can deal with postscript files.

Running costs

With a dot matrix printer, the only regular running costs involved are the costs of paper and printer ribbons. The case with laser printers is different, as the toner cartridges are relatively expensive and must be replaced at regular intervals. This cost should be taken into account when deciding on purchase. Normal paper can be used, but, due to the cost of toner cartridges, each printed sheet will result in a cost of significant size. Another important point is that the laser drum may need replacing eventually; it does not have an unlimited life.

The total running costs of a typical laser printer for a PC may be between 1p and 3p per copy.

Colour

Colour laser printers are available at extra cost, and these may quickly prove popular with businesses and individuals. There is a tendency to want to produce output as good as the best available.

Plotter

This device differs from a conventional printer in that is has been designed mainly for the printing of drawings which have been produced on the computer. Graphic design, architecture and similar industries make great use of plotters. The most common plotters available for personal computers work by moving a pen freely across the paper in order to reproduce the lines stored in the graphic file. The pen may be interchangeable to make coloured drawings possible, or the plotter may be capable of changing to different colours automatically.

■ **Printer drivers**

In order to make a printing device work with a specific program running on the computer, it is necessary to use a program called a printer driver. The user may not necessarily be aware of this, but if there is more than one type of printer available for printing from a particular computer, then the user must select the appropriate printer driver. The drivers for various printers are supplied by the software manufacturer, and are normally installed on the hard disk or network disk drives at the time of installation of the software application itself. The program in use will have an option to choose from a range of different printer drivers. The user should get in the habit of checking before printing any document or other file that the correct printer driver has been selected, or else much time and paper can be wasted.

A different printer driver is needed for each make and model of printer, and for each software application in use. The exception to this is when using a standard interface such as Microsoft Windows. If you have a printer driver for any Windows based program already installed, then this driver should work for any other Windows-based program.

■ **Choosing the right printer for the task**

It is important to select the right printer for the right job. If you are working on a network or even with a stand-alone computer, there will often be more than one printer type to choose from. It is best to reserve a laser printer for final copies of work which has to be of high quality, and use a cheaper faster dot matrix or similar machine for all other work. Typically, on a network, laser printers are available, but a special request may have to be made to send work to them. All other work goes to a dot matrix by default.

If you are producing a document on a word processor, print your draft copy on dot matrix, and only use the laser printer if you are certain that the document is correct and that it has to be printed to a high quality.

14 Integrating applications

Background to integration

Integration is the combining of different applications or programs for a single job or task. An example of integration is the production of a table of figures in a spreadsheet program which is then transferred to a word processor so that comments may be added. The result may be a report.

There are broadly two ways in which the user may integrate applications. First, files can be saved in one application (and they may need to be saved with a special format) and then retrieved from within another application. This generally works well with most current programs, as long as the user takes the trouble to find out the precise format of file which the programs he or she is using will accept. For example, a Lotus 1-2-3 spreadsheet file will export quite readily into the word processor Word Perfect, as long as it is saved with the right format. The user manual or help screens for the applications should be consulted for advice on file formats.

The second method of obtaining integration is where the computer program is itself already integrated, in that it consists of several sub-programs which operate in a similar way and are designed for files and data to be passed easily between them. An example of this is the program Microsoft Works. It consists of a spreadsheet, a database and a word processor, and it is very easy to transfer files and data between the three elements. This type of program is called an integrated package.

▶▶ **FIND OUT**

Find out whether there is an integrated package available on your system. If so, you may use it for the activities which follow in this chapter. If there is no integrated package available, find out how to transfer files between the spreadsheet, word processor and database on your system.

Activity 14.1 Producing a sales report

SITUATION

Produce an analysis on spreadsheet of sales figures, and transfer resulting figures, together with a graph to a word processed report.

CONTENTS

Analyse and present data by spreadsheet analysis; graph figures in a spreadsheet; save files in correct format for transfer to another application; produce a report combining information from a variety of sources.

Levels: INTERMEDIATE, ADVANCED

Elements: PREPARE, PROCESS, PRESENT INFORMATION

TASKS

1 Run the spreadsheet program.

2 Create a spreadsheet model to deal with the following data, which shows the Target (T) sales and Actual (A) sales for the sales managers of the eight different regions of Wessex Windows. The data is for the four quarters of 1993.

QUARTERLY REGIONAL SALES ANALYSIS 1993

		Q1 T	Q1 A	Q2 T	Q2 A	Q3 T	Q3 A	Q4 T	Q4 A
Nigel Williams	Cornwall	25.0	22.9	25.0	22.7	26.0	24.7	28.0	24.4
Jane Andrews	Dorset	34.0	27.3	34.0	28.1	35.0	26.9	37.0	25.0
Joan Davies	Devon	30.0	29.6	30.0	30.0	31.0	30.5	33.0	32.2
Mike Blagg	Somerset	40.0	41.0	40.0	41.5	41.0	41.7	43.0	42.2
Kevin Simons	N. Hants	18.0	11.9	18.0	12.8	19.0	13.7	21.0	15.5
David Wilberforce	S. Hants	18.0	16.0	18.0	17.0	19.0	17.1	21.0	15.9
Heather Shakespeare	N. Wilts	20.0	20.0	20.0	20.3	21.0	20.3	23.0	20.3
Jeremy Jenkins	S. Wilts	20.0	20.5	20.0	19.7	21.0	16.0	23.0	14.9

3 Place a formula at the foot of the Q1 T column to total the targets for all areas. Copy this formula across to the other columns for target and actual sales.

4 Insert two extra columns to the right of each quarter's actual sales.

5 In the first of these new columns, place a formula for the Cornwall area to calculate the difference from target (A–T). Copy the formula down for the other areas.

6 Copy the formulae for this complete column to the columns for the 2nd, 3rd and 4th quarters of 1993.

7 In the second of the newly inserted columns, place a formula for the Cornwall area to calculate actual sales as a percentage of target sales. Copy the formula down for the other areas.

8 Copy the formulae for this complete column to the columns for the 2nd, 3rd and 4th quarters of 1993.

9 Place a formula at the foot of the appropriate columns to calculate the average difference from target (A–T) for each quarter and the average percentage of target achieved for each quarter. Use the average function of the spreadsheet in your formula.

10 Make any changes necessary to the layout, headings, alignment and font sizes in order to produce a clear, concise printout of the data and statistics at this stage. Preview the printout and print a copy.

11 Save the spreadsheet file to your own disk or your own user area under the file name SALESTAT.

12 Draw a multiple bar chart directly from the spreadsheet data to show the percentage of target achieved by each sales rep for each quarter of 1993. This should be done by using the graph function of your spreadsheet program or by exporting the appropriate numbers from the spreadsheet to a program which draws graphs.

13 Place appropriate titles, axis and series labels on the graph. If necessary, save this graph to your own disk or your own user area under the file name SALEGRPH. (This may not be necessary, as some spreadsheet programs automatically save any graphs along with the main spreadsheet file.)

14 In the spreadsheet, copy the sales managers' names and areas to another (currently blank) part of the spreadsheet. Also copy the values (but not the formulae) in the A–T columns, so that you have a table showing only the difference from target for each sales manager.

15 Create a word-processing file consisting of the following elements:

- A title and introduction.
- A table showing the original figures together with the statistics you have calculated. (This should be done by transferring the information from the spreadsheet. Make any adjustments necessary to the transferred information to obtain a satisfactory layout.)
- The graph which shows the percentage of target achieved for each sales manager for each quarter of 1993. (This should be done by transferring the information from the spreadsheet or graph program.)
- Approximately 100 to 150 words of text which summarises the performance of the sales team during 1993.

16 Carefully check the layout and spelling in your report before you save to your own disk or your own user area under the file name SALESREP.

17 Make a back-up copy of the file under a different file name and on a different drive or directory.

18 Print the final version of the report, preferably on a laser or other high output quality printer. In your own handwriting, neatly label the different sections of the report which were produced using different elements of the software (such as word processor, graph program and spreadsheet program).

19 List on screen, and then print on paper, the files in the directories you have used, including the file names for this activity.

20 Exit the programs which are still in use.

Mail merge

All word processors include a facility for carrying out a mail merge. This means that you can produce a standard letter which is to be sent out to a number of people or organisations, with the majority of letters containing standard information, but with certain details changing for each letter.

For example, an organisation might have eight customers whose accounts records show that they owe payments for goods which were purchased more than two months ago. With mail merge, you can place the name and address of the customer at the top of the letter, with the customer's account number and amount owing in the main body of the letter. It is only necessary to design the standard letter once; the computer then merges the standard letter with a list of customers' details.

The precise method of carrying out a mail merge depends upon the word processor program being used, but the general method is as follows:

- Write the standard letter on the word processor.
- Place special filed indicators at positions in the letter where the individual customers' details are to appear.
- Save the mail merge standard letter as a file on disk in the normal way.
- Key in the customers' details as a separate file and store on disk. In some cases these details will be keyed into a database, with one record for each customer and a field for each item to be included in the standard letter. Of course, it is quite likely that the customers' details already exist on file; it may be a matter of selecting the list of customers required from a database program.
- In cases where the customers' details are entered direct to the word processor program, the details may need to be in the same order as that required in the standard letter.
- Give the instruction for the mail merge to take place, specifying the file name of the standard letter and the file name of the customers' details. In some systems, both files will need to be open before the mail merge can take place.

- The letters will now be printed, with the customers' details changing for each letter. The letters should be carefully previewed before printing, to ensure that the layout is correct. In particular, the user should check that varying field lengths for customers' details have not spoilt the layout of the letter.

Activity 14.2 Word processor with mail merge

SITUATION

You are working in the accounts and administration section at Sportstown Leisure Centre. It is time for a batch of members of the centre to renew their membership subscription, and you need to do a mail merge to produce a letter for each customer, requesting the amount owed for the subs. The amounts owed by different members varies, according to the particular facilities they use and the clubs they belong to.

CONTENTS

Carry out a mail merge, combining standard letter with database details; make adjustments required for satisfactory final copies.

Level: ADVANCED

Elements: PREPARE, PROCESS, PRESENT INFORMATION

TASKS

1 Run the word processor program.

2 Enter the following text:

Sportstown Leisure Centre
12 Harvey Road
Sportstown
KN1 3RL

12/04/95

Dear

Member number:

Your annual subscription for membership of the Leisure Centre is due for payment on 1 May 1995. You are currently a full member of the Leisure Centre with the following premium activities at reduced rate:

Payment of the amount due: £   within 14 days of receipt of this letter entitles you to two free activities! In addition, we now have a wider range of activities on offer, including our excellent new, international-standard running and field events track.

Please come in to make you payment, or alternatively, give us a call and we can easily process the payment on your credit card.

Thanks, and we hope to see you soon.

Yours sincerely

Leisure Centre Manager

Note that the Leisure Centre address is centred at the top of the letter, but the rest of the text should be left aligned.

3 Save the letter to your own disk or your own user area under the file name STANDRD1. Make a backup copy of the letter (under a different file name) to guard against accidental loss.

4 Set up, either in the word processor, or in a database file, depending on your system, the following fields:

SURNAME
INITIALS
ADDR1
ADDR2
TOWN
COUNTY
POSTCODE
MEMNUMBER
PREMIUM1
PREMIUM2
PREMIUM3
SUBS

5 Enter the following details for members, noting that some fields for some members will need to be left blank:

D Ching
12 Rowlands Close
Southampton
Hants
SO6 7RT
00234
SQUASH
BADMINTON
27.50

R Hale
11 Stockholm Road
Hedge End
Southampton
SO1 2GR
00279
SQUASH
25.00

N Hayter
6 Osborne Close
Southampton
SO9 3FG
00108
FITNESS
25.00

C Newton
120 Long Road
Southampton
SO4 5GY
00416
20.00

K Smith
18 Cecil Road
Sportstown
Southampton
SO11 4RG
00339
BADMINTON
FITNESS
RUNNING
30.00

6 Save the member details to your own disk or your own user area under the file name MEMBERS1.

7 Retrieve the standard letter, and place field indicators for the following details in the letter:

- the member's name and address, on the left hand side, above the date;
- member number, as indicated in the letter;
- a list of the premium activities for the member, each on a separate line, after '... reduced rate:';
- the amount due, as indicated in the letter.

8 Save the letter under the same file name, overwriting the previous version.

9 Preview the printout of the mail merge letter, make any adjustments necessary in order to obtain satisfactory letters with a suitable layout, and print them.

10 On one of the letters, in your own handwriting, label the information which came from the 'database' part of the software, as distinct from the word processor.

11 List on screen, and then print on paper, the files in the current directory, including the file names for this activity.

12 Exit the word processor and/or database program.

15 Glossary of terms

Absolute cell reference A reference to a spreadsheet cell which is fixed; the same cell is used in a formula, wherever the formula is copied to.

Alignment The way that text is displayed in a spreadsheet cell or database field; it can be left-aligned, right-aligned or centred.

Back-up copy A second copy of a file which is kept for security purposes.

Batch file A file which contains commands or instructions which are carried out in sequence.

Binary The base two-number system which is used by computers for the method of storage of information.

Bulletin board A computer based information system which is available to users who connect to it via telephone lines.

CAD (computer-aided design) The use of a computer for screen based drawing and design work.

CD–ROM (compact disc read only memory) A storage device on optical disc.

Cell One position or box in a spreadsheet.

Co-processor An additional processor chip which can improve the performance of a personal computer.

Communications The use of computers for sending and receiving information to and from other computers.

Conference A computer version of a conference in which delegates to the conference can read other delegates' contributions and make their own through a central computer storage system.

CP/M (control program for microcomputers) A microcomputer operating system.

CPU (central processing unit) The electronic heart of a computer which carries out the storing, processing and controlling functions of the computer.

Cursor A mark on the screen which indicates where a typed character will appear.

Cut-and-paste A method of transferring part of a drawing or document from one area to another.

Data privacy The keeping private of information stored on computer.

Data Protection Act A law which gives rights to data subjects and puts obligations on data users.

Data security The keeping safe of information stored on computer.

Data subject A person whose personal data is stored on computer.

Data user A person or organisation which keeps personal data on computer.

Database A large, structured store of information held on computer, or the software which facilitates this.

Desktop publisher The use of a personal computer for the production of documents which may contain both text and images.

Dictionary A list of words kept in a file for use by a spell checker program.

DOS (disk operating system) The operating system of the majority of personal computers.

Dot matrix printer A printing device which produces its characters by making their shape from a combination of small dots.

Draft printout The first printed copy of a document, which is usually used for checking and amending before production of the final copy.

Electronic mail (Email) A computer messaging system which relies on the storage of messages in central pigeon-holes.

Export To transfer information (usually a file) out of one software application and into another.

Field One piece of information which makes a record on a database file.

File A collection of similar records in a computer database.

File manager A Microsoft Windows program which allows the user to view and manipulate files on a number of disks.

File name extension The extra characters added to the end of a file name in MS–DOS which allows the computer to distinguish files produced in one program from files produced in another.

Floppy disk drive A storage device attached to computers which uses removable 3.5 inch or 5.25 inch plastic disks.

Font A precise set of shapes of printed characters.

Formatting Preparing a blank disk for storage of computer data.

Formula A mathematical combination of the contents of spreadsheet cells or database fields.

Function key One of the keys on a standard keyboard which may be programmed or set up by the user to carry out particular tasks.

Grammar checker A computer program which checks the grammar of the text in a document.

Graphics The use of a computer for the production of drawings, charts or other images.

Hard disk drive The fixed, high-capacity disk drive which is usually contained inside the CPU box of a personal computer.

Hardware Any physical device in computing.

Highlighting Selecting parts of a document or image by pointing to it with the aid of mouse or keyboard.

Icon A small picture which represents a file, program or operation on a computer screen.

Import To transfer information (usually a file) out of one software application and into another.

Index A reference or list which is used by a computer to speed up access to information (usually in relation to a database).

Ink-jet printer A printing device which produces its output by firing small jets of ink at the paper.

Justification of text In a word processor, the alignment of text with the left or right margin (or both margins).

LAN (local area network) A number of computers on one site connected together for the purpose of sharing and communicating information.

Laser printer A printing device capable of high-quality output in which a laser beam controls the production of the image.

Letter quality High-quality printed text.

Log on To become accepted as a genuine user of a computer system.

Mail merge To combine a document file with a list of database files to produce a set of standard documents in which the details vary.

Mainframe computer A powerful computer used by large organisations which may support many users or many applications simultaneously.

Mb (megabyte) A unit of computer storage which is approximately equivalent to a million characters.

MHz (megahertz) A measure of the speed of a computer processor in terms of millions of cycles per second.

Mid-range computer A computer system which, in size and power, is between a personal computer and a mainframe computer.

Modem A device which converts information between computer form and telephone form, used for computer communication through telephone lines.

Monitor A computer screen.

Mouse A desk-based pointing device used in conjunction with computer systems.

MS–DOS (Microsoft Disk Operating System) The standard operating system for personal computer systems.

Near letter quality Medium-quality text output.

Netware An operating system for local area networks.

Network A number of interconnected computers.

Operating system The software required for the user to communicate with the hardware of a computer, either directly, or through an application program.

Optical disc A data device based on optical storage methods.

Organisation chart A chart used in business to show the structure of all or part of an organisation.

OS2 A personal computer operating system produced by IBM.

Overwriting or overtyping Replacing previously typed or stored data with new data.

Palette The set of screen colours in use in a particular application.

Password A code which is required to be entered in conjunction with a USER ID in order to gain entry to all or part of a computer system.

Pentium A particular generation of processor used in personal computers.

Personal computer A standard design of small computer system.

Pigeon-hole A central storage area where messages for users of an electronic mail system are posted.

Pixel A single colour element or dot which, combined with millions of others, makes up the image on a computer monitor.

Plotter A printing device which draws lines.

Pointer A screen arrow which is used in conjunction with a mouse in order to draw or select choices from screen menus.

Presentation A set of charts or text pages which can be used to assist with a verbal presentation of information to an audience.

Printer driver A program which is required for the sending of computer output to a specific printing device.

Processor The electronic heart of a personal computer.

Program A set of instructions stored in a file which carry out a particular task on a computer.

Program manager An element of Microsoft Windows which helps the user to organise and launch application programs running under Windows.

Protocol An agreed or standard format for the transmission of data from one computer to another.

Public domain software Programs which are available to the public, free of charge.

Query A condition, or set of conditions, which enable the user of a database to retrieve specific information.

RAM (random access memory) Computer memory, the contents of which may be changed, and are lost when power is switched off.

Recalculation The calculation of a spreadsheet or database formula, based on changed data.

Record The data referring to a single entity within a database.

Report A file which specifies the precise content and layout of information to be printed from a database.

Resolution The sharpness of a computer monitor, defined by the number of pixels which make up the image.

Retrieve To call up information from a computer storage system.

Save To store information from the current memory of a computer in a file, usually on disk.

Search and replace A feature, usually of word processor programs, which enables the user to search for a string of text and replace all occurrences of it by another string of text.

Select To point to or highlight part of the data in use.

Shareware Computer programs which may be tried out by the user free of charge for a limited period of time, after which they must be paid for if kept.

Software Computer programs.

Sort To change the order of records in a database, or of lines in a spreadsheet or word processor.

Spell checker A program or part of a program which compares words in a document with words in a dictionary, highlights any words which cannot be matched, and suggests corrected spellings.

Spreadsheet A number-based application program in which data is entered into cells (arranged in rows and columns) and contents of cells may be combined by entering mathematical formulae.

SVGA (Super VGA) A particular type of computer monitor.

Template A standard format or layout for a document which can be stored for repeated use.

Thermal printer A printing device which produces its characters by applying heat to heat-sensitive paper.

Thesaurus A feature of a spell checker which gives alternative words of similar meaning.

Tutorial A feature which teaches the use of an application program.

UNIX An operating system used, in different versions, on a range of types of computer systems.

Update To change or bring up to date a computer file.

Upgrading Adding or changing parts of the hardware of a computer system in order to improve performance or capabilities.

UPS (uninterruptible power supply) A piece of electrical equipment which alleviates the effects of power cuts in a computer system.

User ID (user identity or user name) The name of a genuine, recognised user of a secured computer system.

User manual A reference source for the use of a computer program or hardware device.

VGA (video graphics adaptor) A particular type of computer monitor.

Window Part of the computer screen image in which work may be done separate from that in another window.

Word processor A computer program for the production of documents which contain mainly text.

WYSIWYG (what you see is what you get) A description of a screen image which matches closely the version which will be printed on paper.

Index

Access 141
Activity mapping table 20
Autocad 111
Autoexec.bat 136
Autosketch 111

Backup procedure 227, 228, 229
Bit image 256
Bitmap 60
Budget 84, 87
Bulletin board 170
Building floor plans 114

Calculator 136
Calendar 136
Campus 2000 171
Cash flow 82, 83
CD-ROM 245, 246
Central processing unit (CPU) 241, 242, 243, 252
CGA 249
Chart
   area 186
   bar 186, 188, 215
   compound 187
   high/low/close 186, 188, 215
   line 186, 188
   multiple 187
   organisation 186, 188, 189, 215
   pie 186, 188, 215
   scatter 188, 215
   text 186
Charts 186, 187, 188, 189, 190
CIX 171
Click and drag 250
Clipper 141

Clock 137
Co-processor 247
Colour palette 117
Column 60
Communications 168–74
Computer-aided design (CAD) 112
Conferencing 170, 171
Config.sys 136
Copying cell contents 87
Corel Draw 111
Costing 87
CP/M 46
Cut and paste 113

Data 239
   graphical 240
   mixed 240
   numeric 239
   privacy 230, 231
   processing 241
   security 226–30
   textual 240
   transmission 48
Data Protection Act 230, 231
Database 133, 140–9, 259, 263
Dataease 141
Desk Top publishing (DTP) 58–64
Diagram slide 215
Dictionary 25
Disk drive 247
Disk storage 114, 115, 149, 189, 190
Display tablet 217
Drawing 61, 111–9, 186, 187
Dumb terminal 251

EGA 249

Electronic mail (Email) 168, 171–4
Eraser 119
Error checking 169, 170
Errors 48, 227
Excel 81

Field 143, 145
Field type 145
Field
  date 145
  logical 145
  numeric 145
  text 145
  index 147
  program 148
  report 147
  management 49
  manager 135, 250
  names 229
  structure 144, 145
Filed, memo 145
Files 135
Flip 118
Floppy disk 30, 228–30, 240, 244, 245
Floppy disk drive 27, 62
Fonts 26, 61
Forecasts 84
Formula 85, 87
Foxpro 141

Garden design 113
Grammar checker 26
Graphics 61, 111
Graphics card 247
Graphs 87
Grow 118

Hard disk 30, 240
Hard disk drive 27, 62–4, 145
Hard disk storage 245
Hardware 24, 27, 114, 148, 216, 238–258
Harvard graphics 186, 187

Health and safety 223–227
Hercules graphics 249

IBM 243
Icons 133
Image 60, 61
Import 59, 60
Information technology (IT) 238, 239
Input data 47
Integrated package 259
Integration 259, 263
Internet 174
IT
  advantages 238, 239
  disadvantages 238, 239

Kermit 173
Keyboard 27, 62, 249–51
Kitchen design 113

Laptop computer 142
Laser printer 190, 225
Local area network (LAN) 133, 169
Lotus 1-2-3 81
Lotus Ami Pro 25

Mail merge 263
Mailing list 172
Mainframe 251, 252
Memory 48, 49, 256
Microsoft Word 25
Mid-range computer 252
Minicomputer 252
Modem 169, 170
Monitor 27, 29, 62, 63, 115, 148, 189, 225, 248, 249
Mouse 27, 62, 115, 250, 251
MS-DOS 25, 46, 47, 49, 50, 131
Multi-media 217

Near letter quality (NLQ) 253
Notepad 136
Number format 86

Off line 48
Office
   environment 225
   office furniture 224
   layout 114
Operating system 46, 47
Optical disk storage 245, 246
OS/2 46

Page description language 256
Page layout 26, 60
Pagemaker 58
Paint fill 117
Paintbrush 60, 111, 136
Paradox 141
Pentium 244
Personal computer 24, 27, 62
Petty cash 81
Photograph slide 216
Pictures 60
Pixel 63, 114, 249
Plotter 257
Postscript 256, 257
Presentations 213–17
Printer 27, 30, 62, 115, 149, 190
Printer
   bubble-jet 254
   dot matrix 31, 190, 225, 253, 257
   driver 258
   ink-jet 65, 225, 254
   laser 31, 65, 255–257
   thermal 255
Processor 28, 62, 63, 114, 144, 148, 189, 242–4, 247
Processor speed 244
Professional Draw 111
Program manager 132, 133
Protocol 173

Quark XPress 59
Quattro 81

Random access memory (RAM) 46–9, 85, 115, 242, 246, 247

Recalculation 87
Record 143, 146
Records
   add 146
   delete 146
   edit 146
   retrieve 147
   select 147
   sort 146
Roller-ball 251

Screen form 145
Search and replace 27
Serif Page Plus 59
Shareware 170
Shrink 118
SIMMS 247
Slide show 216
Slide show effects 216
Software 24, 187, 226
Spell checker 25, 26
Spray can 118
Spreadsheet 81–7, 132, 134, 259
Standard letter 263
Statistical analysis 84
Storage 240
Sub-directory 49
Super VGA 249
Supercalc 81

Task switching 134
Telephone network 169
Template files 26
Text slide 215
Thesaurus 26
Tilt 118
Transmission 168

Uninterruptible power supply (UPS) 229
Unix 46, 252
Upgrading 246, 247
User group 226
User Id 231

Utilities 133

VAT calculations 82
Ventura Publisher 59
VGA 249
Virus 227

Wide carriage printer 149
Window
　cascade 135
　maximise 134
　minimise 134
　moving 134
　multiple 135
　size 134
　tile 135

Windows 25, 50, 131–17, 248, 250, 258
Windows 95 46, 131, 174
Windows accessories 135
Windows for Workgroups 131
Windows Write 136
Word Perfect 24, 259
Word processor 24, 25, 28, 29, 61, 248, 258, 259, 263
Wordstar 25
World Wide Web 174
WYSIWYG 28, 63, 243

Xmodem 173

Z modem 173